Netiquette

Netiquette™

Virginia Shea

Foreword by
Guy Kawasaki

Albion Books   San Francisco

Albion Books
4547 California St.
San Francisco 94118
info@albion.com

Edition 1.0 / ISBN 0-9637025-1-3
Printed in the United States of America

03 02 01 00 99 98 97 96 95 94 10 9 8 7 6 5 4 3 2 1

To my grandmothers
Helen King Ensinger and Doris Luetkemeyer Shea
and my aunts
Juli Towell and Charlotte Everts

Contents

Foreword

When I die, I am going to have a handful of books placed in my coffin. I need them to ensure for eternity that my grammar is correct, that I'm entertained, and that I'm inspired. The books are:

- *The Chicago Manual of Style*
- *The Elements of Style* (William Strunk, Jr. and E. B. White)
- *Writers on Writing* (Jon Winokur)
- *If You Want to Write* (Brenda Ueland)

Now whoever buries me will have to squeeze one more book into my coffin: *Netiquette* by Virginia Shea. Where I'm going, there will be electronic mail (and it won't be owned by Microsoft). For all eternity, I want to observe the rules that Shea has established for network etiquette.

You're probably standing in the computer section of a bookstore surrounded by too many books about the Internet and the information superhighway. You're confused: Which book do I really need about all this email stuff?

It doesn't matter which of the technical books you buy because they all contain the same *downloaded* files. However, if you want to read a book that was *written* and that teaches you principles that you will use for a long, long time, this is it.

I used to think that network etiquette meant sticking a few smileys in your messages. I wish I had written *Netiquette*. It should be bundled with every modem. It should be mandatory reading for new users of the Internet. I wouldn't print my Internet address here without it.

Guy Kawasaki

Kawasaki@radiomail.net
author of *Hindsights, The Macintosh Way, Selling the Dream, The Computer Curmudgeon,* and *Database 101*

Acknowledgments

Before anyone else, I would like to thank Catherine Hubbard for recognizing that a book on Netiquette needed to be written. Next, I thank my editor and publisher, Seth Ross. Seth asked me to write *Netiquette*, kept after me when I wasn't sure I could do it, discussed Netiquette issues with me, and provided me with tons of source material. He also edited and designed the book and wrote the sections "The Many Domains of Cyberspace" and "The Varieties of Flaming Experience." Seth may well be the first of a new professional breed—the Renaissance publisher.

Many thanks go to my former colleagues at the Electric Power Research Institute, particularly Marie Bergstrom, Renée Morell, and my other friends in the publications department. Our great years working together provided the foundation for the "Business Netiquette" section of this book. And their support and encouragement when I decided to write *Netiquette* were a tremendous inspiration.

I would also like to thank Rich Amlin and the students in his Internet class at Monta Vista High School in Cupertino, particularly Joseph Fieger, Libby Handelsmann, Randy Ksar, Ryan Kubica, Ethan Kuniyoshi, and Michael Nguyen. These students, who know their way around the Internet far better than I do, approach electronic communication with a combination of enjoyment and matter-of-factness that I

13

expect will become the prevailing attitude among computer users. And that's exactly as it should be.

Special thanks to my many online acquaintances. Many of their posted writings—in particular, articles by Jorn Barger, Kay Klier, and Graham Wolff Christian—provided valuable insights. I'd especially like to acknowledge the members of the USENET newsgroup rec.pets.cats, my first lurking ground, and America Online's Melrose Place and Beverly Hills 90210 message boards. I learned about Netiquette first-hand—by making my own mistakes—in these discussion groups.

Thanks to the experts who reviewed the book: M Carling, Daniel Kehoe, David Scalise, and Patrick McEvoy. Their comments beefed up the final product considerably. Thanks also to proofreaders Mae Kaven and Nancy Tune, who saved me many embarrassments. The standard disclaimer holds true here: Any remaining errors are mine alone.

Netiquette was inspired and informed by the work of many other authors. In particular, the general etiquette guidebooks and columns of Judith Martin, better known as Miss Manners, set a standard for etiquette writers that I can only hope to approach. Gene Spafford's excellent online guides to USENET netiquette were a major source for factual information. Guy Kawasaki's *The Macintosh Way* was the first book to show me that a computer book could be funny. Extra special thanks, too, to Guy for writing the foreword to *Netiquette*!

Finally, my deepest thanks and best love go to my husband, Andrew Mendelsohn. He was my best reviewer, collaborator, and supporter throughout the process of writing this book. I might possibly have started on my own, but I would not have finished *Netiquette* without Andrew.

A Note on Terminology

A few terms that might be confusing to some readers are tossed around rather casually in this book. For anyone who's interested, here are explanations of the most important ones:

The Internet, the Matrix, Cyberspace, the net

"The Internet" refers to a worldwide network connecting thousands of university, government, and corporate networks that have all agreed to use a common protocol to communicate with each other.

"The Matrix" refers to all the computers in the world that can exchange electronic mail. It includes the computers on the Internet as well as commercial online services like CompuServe. "Cyberspace" means almost the same thing. It's sort of a psychic superset of the Matrix—it's the psychic space in which people interact when they communicate via computers. "Cyberspace" and "the net" are used synonymously in this book.

Electronic mail, email

Electronic mail, or email, is any message that's directed from one individual to another and is sent from one computer to another. I've spoken to some people who thought it only counted as email if a little flashing icon appeared on your screen when you got mail. Others think of email as Internet mail, which can be used to send email between different organizations, as opposed to LAN (local area network) mail systems that only work within a single organization. The truth is much simpler. If a note was sent from someone else's computer to yours, it's email.

The word email can also be spelled E-mail or e-mail. All three versions are correct.

Email notes and messages

Some email systems differentiate between "notes" and "messages." In this book, the terms are used interchangeably to refer to any communication sent via electronic mail.

Discussion groups

In this book, the term "discussion group" refers to an ongoing written conversation about a given specific topic, to which many people contribute their thoughts. "Discussion groups" include computer discussion forums, message boards, bulletin boards, electronic mailing lists, and USENET newsgroups.

Postings, notes, messages, articles

To participate in a discussion group, you "post" your written thoughts for other participants to read. The posted item may be referred to as a posting, a note, a message, or an article; they all mean approximately the same thing.

Part I

Introduction to Netiquette

1. *When in Cyberspace ...*

The word "etiquette" means "the forms required by good breeding or prescribed by authority to be required in social or official life." Etymologically, it comes from the French word for "ticket." If you know the etiquette for a particular group or society, you have a ticket for entry into it.

To get along in any given society, we're told, "When in Rome, do as the Romans do." But what do you do when Rome is both invisible and divided into dozens of different ethnic neighborhoods, each with its own customs? This Rome, of course, is cyberspace—the mass consensual hallucination in which humans all over the planet meet, converse, and exchange information.[1]

When you send email to your boss, you're in cyberspace. You're in cyberspace when you log into CompuServe or Prodigy, or when you post an article to USENET news. You're in cyberspace when you download a nifty utility or an addictive game from a public server or bulletin board.

In some ways, "cyberspace" is a bad term, because it sounds so mysterious. You're probably not hallucinating when you send an email note

---

1. William Gibson invented the term cyberspace—and this definition for it—in his book *Neuromancer,* the original cyberpunk novel.

to your boss; you're just sitting in your office, typing away, and staring at your computer screen. If you didn't have email, you'd write the note on paper or make a phone call. And when you log into a discussion group, you're not thinking about entering a brave new world; you're probably trying to find out what's wrong with your printer or how to get the fleas off your cat.

Nevertheless, computer networks that let us communicate with people we can't see have created a place that didn't exist before. It's a place that's hard to name or describe, because it exists only in our minds. It's called cyberspace.

The terms "cyberspace," "the net," and "the Matrix" are used interchangeably in this book. John S. Quarterman, an expert in computer communications who coined the term "the Matrix," defines it as all the networked computers in the world that can exchange electronic mail.[2] It includes both the Internet and commercial online services like Prodigy.

Cyberspace contains many different cultures, which some writers have called "virtual communities." Each of these communities has its own rules and customs. But many rules apply throughout almost all of cyberspace. And the purpose of this book is to teach you those rules— to give you a "ticket" to the culture of cyberspace. "Netiquette" is the etiquette of cyberspace.

Q. We can't see people when we talk to them on the phone. Are you trying to tell me I'm entering cyberspace when I call my grandmother in New Jersey?

Actually, at least one writer has defined cyberspace as the place where a telephone call happens.[3] But for most people, "cyberspace" refers to the psychic space where we communicate through computers. Unlike computer networks, telephones have not created communities of people

---

2. Quarterman's book *The Matrix: Computer Networks and Conferencing Systems Worldwide* is an excellent overview of the net (Digital Press, 1990).
3. The great John Perry Barlow, co-founder of the Electronic Frontier Foundation and lyricist for the Grateful Dead.

who otherwise never would have known each other. Usually, when you make a phone call, you know whom you're talking to. (Although I do know a couple who met on the phone. She was working as a telemarketer, selling what later turned out to be vaporware.[4] He returned a couple of calls and finally confessed that he had no interest in her product but would really like to take her out for lunch. They're married now and have an adorable daughter.)

Telephone chat lines serve much the same purpose as network discussion groups. But for some reason—maybe because they're quite expensive, or maybe because the conversation isn't written down and therefore is lost as soon as it's over—they haven't affected our society on the same scale as computer networks.

The culture of amateur radio operation—colloquially known as ham radio—presents a better parallel to cyberspace. For many years, the barriers to becoming a ham and getting on the net were about equivalent. You needed a lot of expensive equipment and specialized knowledge. And, like net mavens of ten or fifteen years ago, hams have their own semi-priestly society based on their shared knowledge and interests. A ham can turn on his radio in the middle of the night and talk to someone on the other side of the country—or the world—and be fairly sure they'll have something in common.

Because the barriers to entering ham culture are still high, the number of hams in the world is still fairly low. But over the last few years, the barriers to entry into cyberspace have dropped dramatically, and the number of people communicating via computers has exploded in a corresponding manner. In fact, today, ham radio operators have their own online discussion groups!

Q. What would I want to do in cyberspace, anyway?

People enter cyberspace—that is, they use computer networks—for two purposes: to communicate with other people and to retrieve informa-

---

4. Vaporware: Software that exists only in the imagination of the marketing department.

tion. This book is concerned largely with the etiquette of communicating with others. Believe it or not, there is also etiquette for information retrieval, and we'll go into that as well.

Most people, once they're networked, spend most of their online time communicating with others. This came as a shock to the founders of Prodigy, who thought their subscribers would want to use the service as a computerized Home Shopping Network. Prodigy's founders—folks at IBM and Sears—based their estimate of how many email messages people would send on the number of paper letters they sent from their home mailboxes. That turned out to be a serious underestimate. A significant number of users started sending far more letters electronically than they ever would have using paper. No one knows exactly why— maybe because it was so much easier than standing in line to buy stamps. Perhaps the Post Office should look into it.

As for why you'd want to communicate via a computer rather than live—there are lots of reasons. Cyberspace communities can put you in touch with experts you'd otherwise never have met. They're also a great place to discuss shared interests. If you're the only twelve-year-old in town who likes opera, you can probably find some compatriots online. You can join a discussion group on almost any topic. And if you can't find a group devoted to a favorite topic, you can start one. Finally, electronic communication is a great way to deal with individuals you can't stand in person. More on this later.

Q. How does one communicate with others via a network?

Several ways. Most cybernauts start with electronic mail (email), which is simply a note typed on a computer and sent over a network to a specific individual or group. The next step for most people is joining discussion groups, in which notes or articles are sent to a central computer for anyone to read. Mailing lists work the same way, except that copies of every note are sent to your electronic mailbox. There are also online "chat" groups, real-time role-playing worlds (often called multi-user dungeons, or MUDs), videoconferencing, virtual reality experiments, and more. New uses are being developed all the time.

Q. Why should I worry about Netiquette? Isn't it all just common sense?

Not all of it. Some rules of Netiquette are based on common courtesy, but have been adapted for a computer culture. Others are based on the technological limits of cyberspace. Still others are matters of convention. Don't ignore these. If you don't bother to learn the conventions of cyberspace, you'll make yourself fair game for flames and bozo filters[5]—a net pariah.

Q. Is Netiquette the same everywhere?

No. Online manners worldwide probably have more in common than, say, table manners. But there are local differences.

For example, among the USENET newsgroups, rec.pets.cats is generally polite, friendly, and helpful, while rec.food.veg sustains virulent flame wars. See "The Art of Flaming" on page 71 for more.

Additionally, some privately owned services (Prodigy, for example) monitor their discussion groups to ensure the content is suitable for a "family audience." (In the case of Prodigy, the result resembles that of similar efforts by the people who run network television. This is not a compliment.)

Any time you enter a new area of cyberspace, it's a good idea to "lurk," or look around, for a while before you say anything. Just log in and read what other people have written before you write anything yourself. That way you'll get an idea of the local mores before you make a fool of yourself.

Despite that disclaimer, most of the rules in this book should apply in most areas of cyberspace.

---

5. *Flames* are angry letters or discussion group postings, usually sent in response to an offensive letter. A *bozo filter* (also called a *kill file*) allows a reader to avoid seeing mail from anyone he or she considers a bozo.

Q. I've been on the net since 1969/1985/1991. Why should I read this book?

Well, it couldn't hurt.

The net right now is a little like New York in the late 19th century—waves of immigrants impinging themselves upon an established society. Not surprisingly, the newcomers don't always behave according to local custom, and members of the old society are sometimes suspicious and resentful. The good news is that newcomers are assimilated much more easily on the net than were the Irish fleeing the potato famine. Most of the residents are friendly, and most of the immigrants only want to please.

Nevertheless, some of the most unpleasant conflicts in cyberspace history have been caused by newcomers who decided to join the fun and, in their ignorance, broke all the rules. This book will give you net oldsters some suggestions on how to help them out.

Q. So who died and made you Queen of Netiquette?

Nobody. I admit it, I'm making it up as I go along.

I've based the rules in this book on personal experience, research, existing online netiquette guides, offline etiquette precedents, and common sense. Despite all efforts to the contrary, there may well be errors or omissions. If you spot one, please let me know via email at the following Internet address: ms.netiquette@albion.com. Naturally, you'll follow the rules proposed in this book for letting others know when they've erred.

2. *The Many Domains of Cyberspace*

Most of the netiquette rules you'll find in this book apply to most areas of cyberspace. Nevertheless, remember that cyberspace is composed of various network domains and services, each with its own character and rules. Currently, cyberspace can be divided into two major domains: the Internet and the commercial online services.

The Internet

Many people have heard of the Internet, but confusion about what it actually is remains. There is a technical definition:

> The Internet is a network of networks all running the TCP/IP protocol suite, connected through gateways, and sharing common name and address spaces.[6]

Don't worry about the "TCP/IP protocol suite" and the rest of the jargon. The key here is the concept of "network of networks." The Internet is not a service per se, like CompuServe or cable TV. Started by the U.S. military in the 1960s, it's evolved into a cooperative arrangement among thousands of university, government, and corporate networks

---

6. This definition is cribbed from Quarterman's *The Matrix*, p. 278.

that have all agreed to use a common protocol for communicating with one another. While the National Science Foundation (NSF) has contributed to its development, no one owns the Internet, and its decision-making is distributed. Most of the services offered on the Internet are free, in keeping with the hacker's credo, "Information wants to be free."

The Internet is vast and sprawling. It's growing so quickly that no one knows exactly how many people actually use it, though an estimated 25-30 million people have access to Internet email. New services are added daily. The lack of central administrative control makes it challenging to use for newcomers and veterans alike. Fortunately, publishers have put out dozens of books about the Internet and its services in the past couple of years. The first of these books, *The Whole Internet User's Guide and Catalog* by Ed Krol, is still the best overall introduction. (See the bibliography for more Internet books.)

Q. What's available on the Internet?

The resources of the Internet grow hourly. The thousands of free public servers on the Internet hold a significant portion of human knowledge, from developments in plasma physics to recipe collections and archives of fine art.[7]

Once you have access to the Internet, you can use a variety of applications to retrieve the information you want. Email connects the Internet to commercial online services and other networks. Mailing lists allow large numbers of email subscribers to maintain running discussions on topics of special interest, from schizophrenia to Slovakian politics. USENET news is a riotous assortment of discussion groups ("newsgroups") that you can browse and contribute to. Telnet allows you to log into remote servers over the Internet. FTP (File Transfer Protocol) is a simple file transfer tool that lets you download information, often anonymously.

---

7. For an excellent guide to Internet and other cyberspace resources, pick up *Net-Guide*, from Random House Electronic Publishing.

The development of new applications constantly fuels the growth of the Internet. Many of these applications have "graphical user interfaces" that make Internet access easy. Free programs like Mosaic, Lynx, and Cello allow you to browse the World Wide Web (WWW), a vast collection of electronic libraries. Hundreds of organizations "publish" and link their works on the WWW. By clicking a mouse button or hitting an arrow key, you can "net surf" from server to server and topic to topic.

Q. How can I get on the Internet?

Most people access the Internet through work or school. The only tools required—at school, work, or home—are a computer, a modem, basic communications software, and a phone line. There are hundreds of companies that sell and resell Internet access, many of them running out of lofts and basements and serving local neighborhoods. Many of these businesses will hold your hand while you're getting started on the Internet. For a list of Internet service providers, see the forthcoming *Internet Now!* from Albion Books.

Acceptable use

The Internet is composed of many networks, each with its own specific rules and usage policies. One of the most important documents in determining Internet rules is the NSFNET Acceptable Use Policy (AUP), which basically restricts use of the NSFNET Internet "backbone" to research, academic, and government uses. It expressly forbids commercial activity unrelated to research.

The AUP doesn't apply, however, to the fastest-growing segments of the Internet run by commercial Internet service providers like PSI, UUNET, and Netcom. In 1990, these providers formed a non-profit organization, the Commercial Internet Exchange (CIX), that is dedicated to carrying commercial Internet traffic.

Q. What's USENET?

USENET is sort of a cross between a campus coffeehouse and a cooperative news service. Although it's closely associated with the Internet, USENET runs on non-Internet systems as well. It's composed of thousands of running discussions called "newsgroups," which are sent to thousands of computers around the world each day. References to "discussion groups" in this book include USENET newsgroups as well as electronic mailing lists and discussion forums on commercial services.

Commercial online services

Several large online services have staked out claims to cyberspace over the past several years. Unlike the Internet, these systems are under corporate control, and their rules are usually quite specific.

CompuServe

CompuServe claims to be "the world's largest commercial computer network." With over 1.5 million subscribers, CompuServe probably offers the best low-cost tech support in the world. If you have a computer question, you post it in the appropriate forum, and within hours you have dozens of answers, many of them correct. There are forums on practically every computer software package ever sold. CompuServe forums are among the best places to get expert information on almost any topic from gardening to copyright law.

CompuServe also gives you email, of course, with an Internet gateway. However, you're charged for messages and files you receive as well as those you send. In fact, you'll find that CompuServe access charges can quickly break a family networking budget, leading to the service's net nickname: Compu$erve.

America Online

America Online was the first specifically Mac-oriented network, though it is now used by hundreds of thousands of PC folk as well. The service comes with its own software, with an easy-to-use graphical user interface. Its other major characteristic is its extreme niceness. The introductory material describes it as an "online community," and most of the people who participate are so darn friendly that it sometimes gets hard to take.

In addition to plenty of useful information, America Online offers "chat rooms" where you can have a written conversation with other people in real time. If you meet someone you like, you can even go off to a "private room." These can be used socially, or as a substitute for a business conference call. But their most common use is for romance—sometimes innocent, often explicitly sexual.

America Online has been growing rapidly, both in terms of the number of subscribers (over 600,000) and in terms of the services it offers. The service set up an Internet mail gateway in 1993, followed by full USENET access in 1994.

Prodigy

Prodigy is the network everyone loves to hate. At a recent talk by Ted Nelson, one of the grand old men of cyberspace, the mere mention of Prodigy got a huge laugh from the audience. The service sells one-fifth of every screen to advertisers, and its unofficial motto is said to be "Shut up and shop."

Owned by IBM and Sears, Prodigy first became notorious for censoring its discussion groups. In their effort to maintain Prodigy's "family" status, censors deleted anything Queen Victoria might have considered remotely inappropriate. An example: Members of the dog fanciers' forum are not allowed to use the word "bitch" to refer to a female dog.

Eventually, discussion group members started using mailing lists to send private, uncensored mail to their network buddies. With almost no warning, Prodigy started charging extra for email usage, making the mailing lists economically unfeasible for many users. Prodigy's explanation: "We never promised to maintain free email service forever."

For years Prodigy said it would never offer an Internet gateway, but in 1993 it finally broke down. However, Prodigy users are charged not only for the Internet messages they send, but also for those they receive. Users are not thrilled.

Despite these drawbacks, Prodigy has a large installed base—over two million users. (It's hard to track exact numbers because the service allows up to six users per subscription.) As a "family" network, Prodigy does have its uses. It's probably used by more kids than most of the other services. I know a junior high school student who wanted to do a report on China's Silk Road and couldn't find anything in the local public library. He posted a query on Prodigy, and got a response from a college student 1500 miles away, with tons of useful information.

The WELL

Started by the folks from the Whole Earth Review, the WELL (Whole Earth 'Lectronic Link) is known for the quality and intimacy of its discussion groups. As one of the smallest services, it has a communal feel missing in the garish screens and corporate orientation of its bigger, more commercial siblings. The WELL is fully connected to the Internet.

Other online services

There are several other commercial services that offer varying degrees of connectivity to the net, including DELPHI, AppleLink, BIX and GENIE. Expect more to be started in the coming months, including eWorld from Apple Computer. Keep in mind that each of these systems has its own rules and usage guidelines.

Part II
Netiquette Basics

THE CORE RULES

Rule 1. Remember the human.

Never forget that the person reading your mail or posting is, indeed, a person, with feelings that can be hurt.

Corollary 1 to Rule #1: It's not nice to hurt other people's feelings.

Corollary 2: Never mail or post anything you wouldn't say to your reader's face.

Corollary 3: Notify your readers when flaming.

Rule 2. Adhere to the same standards of behavior online that you follow in real life.

Corollary 1: Be ethical.

Corollary 2: Breaking the law is bad Netiquette.

Rule 3. Know where you are in cyberspace.

Corollary 1: Netiquette varies from domain to domain.

Corollary 2: Lurk before you leap.

Rule 4. Respect other people's time and bandwidth.

Corollary 1: It's OK to think that what you're doing at the moment is the most important thing in the universe, but don't expect anyone else to agree with you.

Corollary 2: Post messages to the appropriate discussion group.

Corollary 3: Try not to ask stupid questions on discussion groups.

Corollary 4: Read the FAQ (Frequently Asked Questions) document.

Corollary 5: When appropriate, use private email instead of posting to the group.

Corollary 6: Don't post subscribe, unsubscribe, or FAQ requests.

Corollary 7: Don't waste expert readers' time by posting basic information.

OF NETIQUETTE

Corollary 8: If you disagree with the premise of a particular discussion group, don't waste the time and bandwidth of the members by telling them how stupid they are. Just stay away.

Corollary 9: Conserve bandwidth when you retrieve information from a host or server.

Rule 5. Make yourself look good online.

Corollary 1: Check grammar and spelling before you post.

Corollary 2: Know what you're talking about and make sense.

Corollary 3: Don't post flame-bait.

Rule 6. Share expert knowledge.

Corollary 1: Offer answers and help to people who ask questions on discussion groups.

Corollary 2: If you've received email answers to a posted question, summarize them and post the summary to the discussion group.

Rule 7. Help keep flame wars under control.

Corollary 1: Don't respond to flame-bait.

Corollary 2: Don't post spelling or grammar flames.

Corollary 3: If you've posted flame-bait or perpetuated a flame war, apologize.

Rule 8. Respect other people's privacy.

Don't read other people's private email.

Rule 9. Don't abuse your power.

The more power you have, the more important it is that you use it well.

Rule 10. Be forgiving of other people's mistakes.

You were a network newbie once too!

3. *Core Rules of Netiquette*

So you got a modem and a network subscription for your birthday and you want to make some new online friends. Where do you start?

Rule 1: Remember the human

The golden rule your parents and your kindergarten teacher taught you was pretty simple: Do unto others as you'd have others do unto you. Imagine how you'd feel if you were in the other person's shoes. Stand up for yourself, but try not to hurt people's feelings.

In cyberspace, we state this in an even more basic manner:

Remember the human.

When you communicate electronically, all you see is a computer screen. You don't have the opportunity to use facial expressions, gestures, and tone of voice to communicate your meaning; words—lonely written words—are all you've got. And that goes for your correspondent as well.

When you're holding a conversation online—whether it's an email exchange or a response to a discussion group posting—it's easy to misinterpret your correspondent's meaning. And it's frighteningly easy to forget that your correspondent is a person with feelings more or less like your own.

It's ironic, really. Computer networks bring people together who'd otherwise never meet. But the impersonality of the medium changes that meeting to something less—well, less personal. Humans exchanging email often behave the way some people behind the wheel of a car do: They curse at other drivers, make obscene gestures, and generally behave like savages. Most of them would never act that way at work or at home. But the interposition of the machine seems to make it acceptable.

The message of Netiquette is that it's not acceptable. Yes, use your network connections to express yourself freely, explore strange new worlds, and boldly go where you've never gone before. But remember the Prime Directive of Netiquette: *Those are real people out there.*

Would you say it to the person's face?

Writer and Macintosh evangelist Guy Kawasaki tells a story about getting email from some fellow he's never met. Online, this fellow tells Guy that he's a bad writer with nothing interesting to say.

Unbelievably rude? Yes, but unfortunately, it happens all the time in cyberspace.

Maybe it's the awesome power of being able to send mail directly to a well-known writer like Guy. Maybe it's the fact that you can't see his face crumple in misery as he reads your cruel words. Whatever the reason, it's incredibly common.

Guy proposes a useful test for anything you're about to post or mail: Ask yourself, "Would I say this to the person's face?" If the answer is no, rewrite and reread. Repeat the process till you feel sure that you'd feel as comfortable saying these words to the live person as you do sending them through cyberspace.

Of course, it's possible that you'd feel great about saying something extremely rude to the person's face. In that case, Netiquette can't help you. Go get a copy of *Miss Manners' Guide to Excruciatingly Correct Behavior.*

Another reason not to be offensive online

When you communicate through cyberspace—via email or on discussion groups—your words are written. And chances are they're stored somewhere where you have no control over them. In other words, there's a good chance they can come back to haunt you.

Never forget the story of famous email user Oliver North. Ollie, you'll remember, was a great devotee of the White House email system, PROFS. He diligently deleted all incriminating notes he sent or received. What he didn't realize was that, somewhere else in the White House, computer room staff were equally diligently backing up the mainframe where his messages were stored. When he went on trial, all those handy backup tapes were readily available as evidence against him.

You don't have to be engaged in criminal activity to want to be careful. Any message you send could be saved or forwarded by its recipient. You have no control over where it goes.

Rule 2: Adhere to the same standards of behavior online that you follow in real life

In real life, most people are fairly law-abiding, either by disposition or because we're afraid of getting caught. In cyberspace, the chances of getting caught sometimes seem slim. And, perhaps because people sometimes forget that there's a human being on the other side of the computer, some people think that a lower standard of ethics or personal behavior is acceptable in cyberspace.

The confusion may be understandable, but these people are mistaken. Standards of behavior may be *different* in some areas of cyberspace, but they are not *lower* than in real life.

Be ethical

Don't believe anyone who says, "The only ethics out there are what you can get away with." This is a book about manners, not about ethics. But if you encounter an ethical dilemma in cyberspace, consult the code you follow in real life. Chances are good you'll find the answer.

One more point on Netiquette ethics: If you use shareware, pay for it. Paying for shareware encourages more people to write shareware. The few dollars probably won't mean much to you, and they benefit all of cyberspace in the long run.

Breaking the law is bad Netiquette

If you're tempted to do something that's illegal in cyberspace, chances are it's also bad Netiquette.

Some laws are obscure or complicated enough that it's hard to know how to follow them. And in some cases, we're still establishing how the law applies to cyberspace. Two examples are the laws on privacy (see Rule 8 and "Email Privacy—a Grand Illusion" on page 125) and copyright (see "Copyright in Cyberspace" on page 133).

Again, this is a book on manners, not a legal manual. But Netiquette mandates that you do your best to act within the laws of society and cyberspace.

Rule 3: Know where you are in cyberspace

Netiquette varies from domain to domain

What's perfectly acceptable in one area may be dreadfully rude in another. For example, in most TV discussion groups, passing on idle gossip is perfectly permissible. But throwing around unsubstantiated rumors in a journalists' mailing list will make you very unpopular there.

And because Netiquette is different in different places, it's important to know where you are. Thus the next corollary:

Lurk before you leap

When you enter a domain of cyberspace that's new to you, take a look around. Spend a while listening to the chat or reading the archives. Get a sense of how the people who are already there act. Then go ahead and participate.

Rule 4: Respect other people's time and bandwidth

It's a cliché that people today seem to have less time than ever before, even though (or perhaps because) we sleep less and have more labor-saving devices than our grandparents did. When you send email or post to a discussion group, you're taking up other people's time (or hoping to). It's your responsibility to ensure that the time they spend reading your posting isn't wasted.

The word "bandwidth" is sometimes used synonymously with time, but it's really a different thing. Bandwidth is the information-carrying capacity of the wires and channels that connect everyone in cyberspace. There's a limit to the amount of data that any piece of wiring can carry at any given moment—even a state-of-the-art fiber-optic cable. The word "bandwidth" is also sometimes used to refer to the storage capacity of a host system. When you accidentally post the same note to the same newsgroup five times, you are wasting both time (of the people who check all five copies of the posting) and bandwidth (by sending repetitive information over the wires and requiring it to be stored somewhere).

You are not the center of cyberspace

Presumably, this reminder will be superfluous to most readers. But I include it anyway, because when you're working hard on a project and deeply involved in it, it's easy to forget that other people have concerns other than yours. So don't expect instant responses to all your questions, and don't assume that all readers will agree with—or care about—your passionate arguments.

Rules for discussion groups

Rule 4 has a number of implications for discussion group users. Most discussion group readers are already spending too much time sitting at the computer; their significant others, families, and roommates are drumming their fingers, wondering when to serve dinner, while those network maniacs are catching up on the latest way to housebreak a puppy or cook zucchini.

And many news-reading programs are slow, so just opening a posted note or article can take a while. Then the reader has to wade through all the header information to get to the meat of the message. No one is pleased when it turns out not to be worth the trouble. See "Netiquette for Discussion Groups" on page 65 for detailed rules.

To whom should messages be directed? (Or why "mailing list" could become a dirty word)

In the old days, people made copies with carbon paper.[1] You could only make about five legible copies. So you thought good and hard about who you wanted to send those five copies to.

Today, it's as easy to copy practically anyone on your mail as it is not to. And we sometimes find ourselves copying people almost out of habit. In general, this is rude. People have less time than ever today, precisely because they have so much information to absorb. Before you copy people on your messages, ask yourself whether they really need to know. If the answer is no, don't waste their time. If the answer is maybe, think twice before you hit the send key.

Rule 5: Make yourself look good online

Take advantage of your anonymity

I don't want to give the impression that the net is a cold, cruel place full of people who just can't wait to insult each other. As in the world at large, most people who communicate online just want to be liked. Networks—particularly discussion groups—let you reach out to people you'd otherwise never meet. And *none of them can see you.* You won't be judged by the color of your skin, eyes, or hair, your weight, your age, or your clothing.

---

1. For readers who don't remember carbon paper: It's like the black stuff they put between the sheets of your Visa receipt, only in 8 1/2" x 11" pages. People used to put it between sheets of typing paper and make their copies at the same time as the original. It saved a lot of time at the copier, which was an especially good thing given that hardly anyone had copiers.

You will, however, be judged by the quality of your writing. For most people who choose to communicate online, this is an advantage; if they didn't enjoy using the written word, they wouldn't be there. So spelling and grammar do count.[2]

If you're spending a lot of time on the net and you're shaky in these areas, it's worth brushing up on them. There are plenty of books available, but you'll learn more—and possibly have more fun—if you take a course. If you're an older adult,[3] you don't have to take a "bonehead grammar" course with a bunch of bored teenagers. Instead, look for courses on proofreading and copyediting; they usually cover the basic rules of grammar pretty thoroughly, and they'll be filled with motivated students who are there because they want to be. Check your local community college and university extension catalogs—you'll be amazed at what they offer. A side benefit is that taking courses involves meeting people you can actually see.

Know what you're talking about and make sense

Pay attention to the content of your writing. Be sure you know what you're talking about—when you see yourself writing "it's my understanding that" or "I believe it's the case," ask yourself whether you really want to post this note before checking your facts. Bad information propagates like wildfire on the net. And once it's been through two or three iterations, you get the same distortion effect as in the party game "Operator": Whatever you originally said may be unrecognizable. (Of course, you could take this as a reason not to worry about the accuracy of your postings. But you're only responsible for what you post yourself, not for what anyone else does with it.)

---

2. Actually, there's a controversy on the net—not exactly raging, but ongoing—over how important these issues are. Some people believe that electronic communication should be spontaneous and from-the-hip. They don't think anyone should worry about spelling or grammar. Others feel it's worthwhile to think before you post, and that bad spelling and grammar make a bad impression. Obviously, I belong to the second group. However, spelling and grammar flames are *always* bad form. See Rule 7.
3. 23 or older, or out of school for two or more years.

In addition, make sure your notes are clear and logical. It's perfectly possible to write a paragraph that contains no errors in grammar or spelling, but still makes no sense whatsoever. This is most likely to happen when you're trying to impress someone by using a lot of long words that you don't really understand yourself. Trust me—no one worth impressing will be impressed. It's better to keep it simple.

Don't post flame-bait

Finally, be pleasant and polite. Don't use offensive language, and don't be confrontational for the sake of confrontation. See "The Art of Flaming" on page 71 for details.

Q. Is swearing acceptable on the net?

Only in those areas where sewage is considered an art form, e.g., the USENET newsgroup alt.tasteless. Usually, if you feel that cursing in some form is required, it's preferable to use amusing euphemisms like "effing" and "sugar." You may also use the classic asterisk filler—for example, s***. The archness is somehow appropriate to the net, and you avoid offending anyone needlessly. And everyone will know exactly what you mean.

Rule 6: Share expert knowledge

Finally, after all that negativity, some positive advice.

The strength of cyberspace is in its numbers. The reason asking questions online *works* is that a lot of knowledgeable people are reading the questions. And if even a few of them offer intelligent answers, the sum total of world knowledge increases. The Internet itself was founded and grew because scientists wanted to share information. Gradually, the rest of us got in on the act.

So do your part. Despite the long lists of no-no's in this book, you do have something to offer. Don't be afraid to share what you know.

It's especially polite to share the results of your questions with others. When you anticipate that you'll get a lot of answers to a question, or when you post a question to a discussion group that you don't visit often, it's customary to request replies by email instead of to the group. When you get all those responses, write up a summary and post it to the discussion group. That way, everyone benefits from the experts who took the time to write to you.

If you're an expert yourself, there's even more you can do. Many people freely post all kinds of resource lists and bibliographies, from lists of online legal resources to lists of popular UNIX books. If you're a leading participant in a discussion group that lacks a FAQ, consider writing one. If you've researched a topic that you think would be of interest to others, write it up and post it. See "Copyright in Cyberspace" on page 133 for a few words on the copyright implications of posting research.

Sharing your knowledge is fun. It's a long-time net tradition. And it makes the world a better place.

Rule 7: Help keep flame wars under control

"Flaming" is what people do when they express a strongly held opinion without holding back any emotion. It's the kind of message that makes people respond, "Oh come on, tell us how you *really* feel." Tact is not its objective.

Does Netiquette forbid flaming? Not at all. Flaming is a longstanding network tradition (and Netiquette never messes with tradition). Flames can be lots of fun, both to write and to read. And the recipients of flames sometimes deserve the heat.

But Netiquette does forbid the perpetuation of flame *wars*—series of angry letters, most of them from two or three people directed toward each other, that can dominate the tone and destroy the camaraderie of a discussion group. It's unfair to the other members of the group. And while flame wars can initially be amusing, they get boring very quickly to people who aren't involved in them. They're an unfair monopolization of bandwidth.

For advice on sending and receiving flames, see "The Art of Flaming" on page 71.

Rule 8: Respect other people's privacy

Of course, you'd never dream of going through your colleagues' desk drawers. So naturally you wouldn't read their email either.

Unfortunately, a lot of people would. This topic actually rates a separate section. For now, here's a cautionary tale. I call it

The case of the snoopy foreign correspondent

In 1993, Michael Hiltzik, a highly regarded foreign correspondent in the Moscow bureau of the *Los Angeles Times*, was caught reading his coworkers' email. His colleagues became suspicious when system records showed that someone had logged in to check their email at times when they knew they hadn't been near the computer. So they set up a sting operation. They planted false information in messages from another one of the paper's foreign bureaus. Hiltzik read the notes and later asked colleagues about the false information. Bingo! As a disciplinary measure, he was immediately reassigned to another position at the paper's Los Angeles bureau.

The moral: Failing to respect other people's privacy is not just bad Netiquette. It could also cost you your job.

Rule 9: Don't abuse your power

Some people in cyberspace have more power than others. There are wizards in MUDs (multi-user dungeons), experts in every office, and system administrators in every system.

Knowing more than others, or having more power than they do, does not give you the right to take advantage of them. For example, sysadmins should never read private email.

For more on the abuse of power in the milieu of computer networks, see "Egregious Netiquette Violations" on page 83. For more about privacy, see "Email Privacy: a Grand Illusion?" on page 125.

Rule 10: Be forgiving of other people's mistakes

Everyone was a network newbie once. And not everyone has had the benefit of reading this book. So when someone makes a mistake—whether it's a spelling error or a spelling flame, a stupid question or an unnecessarily long answer—be kind about it. If it's a minor error, you may not need to say anything. Even if you feel strongly about it, think twice before reacting. Having good manners yourself doesn't give you license to correct everyone else.

If you do decide to inform someone of a mistake, point it out politely, and preferably by private email rather than in public. Give people the benefit of the doubt; assume they just don't know any better. And never be arrogant or self-righteous about it. Just as it's a law of nature that spelling flames always contain spelling errors, notes pointing out Netiquette violations are often examples of poor Netiquette.

4. *Introduction to Electronic Mail*

Electronic mail is known for its informality. This is partly because of the hacker culture whence email springs and partly because email is so easy to send. In some ways email has more in common with phone discussion than with paper memos, which are traditionally more formal in tone.

Because email communications are written, they can be much more detailed than a phone conversation. And they're delivered almost instantaneously, rather than overnight. So colleagues or friends can have a long "conversation"—with a written record of what they said—over the course of a day.

Anatomy of an email message

When you receive an Internet email message, it usually contains many lines of incomprehensible gibberish before the beginning of the actual text.[1] This chunk of gibberish is known as the "header" of the message. Most of it is a record of the path the message took from the sender's computer to yours. It's useful only when an email message gets lost or

---

1. The text may also be incomprehensible gibberish, but that's a separate issue.

misdelivered; normally, you can safely ignore it. Headers also often contain useful stuff like a time and date stamp and an indication of whether files are attached to the message.

The three most important pieces of information in the header are the email addresses of the sender and the recipient, and a subject line that tells what the message is about. All email messages—whether or not they travel over the Internet—contain these three pieces of information.

When you send an email message, your return address usually appears automatically. You just need to fill in the "To" line (with the recipient's email address) and the "Subject" line (with a clear and concise description of the subject of your message).

The Internet addressing scheme

Internet addresses always take the form "name@organization.domain". For example, my Internet address is

   ms.netiquette@albion.com

The "ms.netiquette" part is my "handle" —my Internet nickname. "Albion," the organization name, refers to Albion Books, my publisher; and "com," the domain designation, means that "Albion" is a commercial business. There are six major Internet domain designations:

com	commercial businesses
edu	educational institutions
org	nonprofit organizations
net	networks
mil	the military
gov	government entities

President Bill Clinton's Internet address is president@whitehouse.gov. Vice President Al Gore's is vice.president@whitehouse.gov. They both welcome email suggestions. Go ahead—give it a try!

Other addressing schemes

Each commercial service and mail system has its own addressing scheme. For example, on CompuServe, people don't have "handles."

Their email addresses are all numbers. Long numbers. Most up-to-date systems allow users to choose their own handles, which makes life a lot easier for everyone who lacks a photographic memory.

Most email systems have Internet gateways. That means you can send mail via the Internet to people who use different email systems or services. Usually, the address within the service is translated to an Internet address. For example, if your CompuServe address was 12345,6789, your friends on CompuServe would just send their mail to 12345,6789. But, because I'm not on CompuServe, I'd have to use the address 12345,6789@compuserve.com.

Email address changes

People's email addresses tend to change fairly frequently. This can happen because of changes in a person's job, in a company's mail system, or in an individual's online service. For example, when Bill Clinton leaves the presidency, you probably won't be able to reach him at president@whitehouse.gov any more.

There isn't much you can do about this except be aware of it. If you have an electronic address book where you store frequently used email addresses, occasionally check the headers of email you receive to make sure all your information is up-to-date.

Q. My email system displays a great big window on my screen/beeps loudly/displays a little flashing icon every time I get mail. Does Netiquette require me to read every message the moment I receive it?

Certainly not. One of the great things about email is that you don't have to interrupt what you're doing to deal with it the way you do for a telephone call. As long as you're checking your mail regularly (daily for home users, two to four times a day for business users), you're practicing good Netiquette.

Most of those notifiers can be turned off if they annoy you. If you don't know how to do it, check with your email system administrator.

Of course, some of us have attention spans so short that we welcome the interruption of email. And an immediate response is very impressive to many people—they think it means you're right on top of your work. If you prefer to read every message as soon as you notice it, go for it. You'll find that more and more of your work gets done via the mail system rather than the phone.

Those wacky email features

Email is full of useful features that, in many cases, didn't exist before. As with paper memos, you can carbon copy (cc) or blind carbon copy (bcc) your notes to anyone on your mail network. You can attach return receipts to your notes so that you'll know when your email has been opened. You can schedule tickler messages months ahead of time. You can flag your messages as "urgent"; in many cases, these notes will appear immediately on the reader's screen. And, on some systems, you can set up a "bozo filter" or "kill file" that automatically screens out email from people whose messages you deem unworthy of reading. All these features vary from system to system.

Carbon copy (cc) and blind carbon copy (bcc)

Use these features anywhere you'd use them when sending a paper memo—for example, when your boss has delegated a project to you and you want to keep her up-to-date on it, or when you request information from a higher-up and want to be sure his secretary also knows about your request. A few carbon copy don'ts:

- Don't cc Steve Jobs on your analysis of the war in Bosnia.

- Don't cc Michael Spindler on your hatchet job about Steve Jobs and John Sculley.

- Don't cc your boss on your lunch date with your friend in Accounts Payable.

In other words, don't waste other people's time.

Return receipts

A receipt is a message the email system sends to the writer of a note after the note has been opened. In *The Computer Curmudgeon,* Guy Kawasaki claims that "receipts are insulting. You are saying to the recipient: 'You're a lazy schlub who never reads his email.'"

Guy has a point, but he goes a little too far. First of all, there *are* lazy schlubs who never read their email. (See "Email overload—imagined" on page 95.) Second, using a receipt is a really good idea when you're not sure whether the email system is working. Where I used to work, the gateway between the Mac mail system and the PC mail system went down all the time. Eventually, I started using a return receipt any time I sent important mail to a PC user because that was the only way I'd know whether the mail had gone through.

Receipts are also useful when you're dealing with high-level executives who are generally good about checking their email but have crazy travel and meeting schedules. If the note isn't read in a reasonable amount of time, you can follow up with a phone call and check whether it was received.

Some systems tell the recipient that you're getting a return receipt and some don't. The ones that notify the mail recipient are practicing better Netiquette.

Prescheduled "ticklers": Friendly reminder or Orwellian control mechanism?

Some systems allow you to write a note months ahead of time and schedule it to be sent later. You could use this feature, for example, to remind yourself to buy your mom a birthday present. Your manager could use it to remind you and your colleagues that an important deadline is approaching. But you wouldn't necessarily know whether he'd written it yesterday or six months ago. On the other hand, you could tell the boss you're working at home, schedule a "progress report" message to be sent off at 3:00 p.m., and take off for the beach.

Netiquette's call on prescheduled ticklers is that the technology is value-neutral; it all depends on how it's used. No manager should use electronic communication to replace human interaction. That's bad Netiquette and bad management. It's both dishonest and rude to claim that a message that was actually written months ago was written today. And using technology to pretend to be somewhere when you're not is inappropriate, no matter who does it.

On the other hand, any technique that helps projects stay on schedule deserves consideration in the business world. In any case, smart employees will probably figure out pretty quickly which messages were sent live and which were written months ago.

The "urgent" flag

Avoid using the "urgent" flag unless your message is both important and time-critical. It's a real irritation to read a note with an urgent flag and discover that it's (a) completely routine or (b) something that can wait a day or more. Some systems will display a message flagged as "urgent" on the recipient's computer screen immediately, but be aware that this feature can usually be defeated.

"Bozo filters" and intelligent filters

In many discussion groups, you can set up a "bozo filter" or "kill file," which automatically screens out notes from people whose messages you deem unworthy of reading. Some companies are now implementing this feature on their corporate email systems.

Bozo filters pose no problem on recreational discussion groups. But you'd want to be very careful using one on your work email system. Say Joe Schmoe down the hall has a bad habit of sending the Blonde Joke of the Day to everyone on the hallway. Since you're a blonde, you don't appreciate this, and you decide to filter all of Joe's mail. But one day, the department director asks Joe to delegate an important project to you. What are you going to say six weeks later when the director wanders into your office to check on the project—"Uh, I never read Joe's email because he's a jerk"? Bad idea.

A better kind of filter allows you to prioritize your mail rather than filtering it completely. For example, mail from your boss or colleagues working on an important project might be top priority; mail from mailing lists might be third or fourth priority.

When to send files (and when not to)

Many email systems allow you to attach files to your email notes. This is a handy feature for the sender, but under some circumstances, a pain in the neck for the receiver, especially if he doesn't have the right tools to access the file. Even under the best circumstances, reading an email note, then saving and opening a file takes significantly longer than just reading an email note. So you should never send a file when a simple note would do.

An example: Occasionally, I used to receive email notes saying only "see attachment." The attachment would invariably turn out to be the word processing file for a paper memo announcing a meeting. It would have been a lot easier for me—and everyone else who received the file—if the relevant information had simply been copied into the email note itself. And copying that information into the note would hardly have taken the sender any longer than sending the file.

On the other hand, the ability to transmit files is a godsend when your file contains important formatting (boldface, italics, et cetera) or other non-text information (a spreadsheet, for example). That's because many email systems allow only ASCII text in their notes, but attached files can contain any kind of information. You can also send a file that's too long to paste into an email note.

All these situations are most likely to arise when both you and your correspondent are working with the files in question. For example, I sent *Netiquette* to my publisher in the form of files rather than email notes because (1) it contained important formatting information and (2) it was long.

When you send a file, it's important to make sure that your correspondent has the application software necessary to open the file. If you're "uuencoding" your file (an Internet standard), make sure your recipient can "uudecode" it. And check whether her version of the software is older than yours. There's nothing more frustrating than trying to open up, say, a PageMaker file, and discovering that your correspondent has already upgraded to the brand-new version while you're still using the old one.

Finally, it's a good idea to include your email address within any file you send. It's a courtesy—just like putting your return address at the top of your letter, as well as on the outside of the envelope, which might get thrown out.

Email flames

Like many other cyberspace travelers, email writers sometimes forget the Golden Rule of Netiquette—Remember the human—and write things they would never say out loud.

Here's a sample situation: A colleague has just used email to respond to some written work you did. The note doesn't just disagree with the point of view you took up; it attacks you in rather personal terms. You're upset. How do you respond?

It takes a little courage, but it's not difficult. First, wait a few hours— even a day or two—to cool down. Then reply to your colleague's note. Say that, while you respect his right to disagree with you, you want him to know that his personal comments hurt your feelings. If you choose, you may also use this note to reply to the substance of his criticisms, but it's probably better to wait. This approach usually brings the discourse back where it belongs—to the substance of the issues, rather than the morals and personal habits of the people in the discussion. It works because it reminds your colleague that you're a human being who deserves to be treated with respect—even over the network.

Of course, if your colleague is the kind of subhuman scum who will never get that message, just flame back. ;-)[2]

Email as a substitute for live interaction

People will occasionally say things like "Electronic communication is no substitute for human interaction." Hogwash. Of course it is. Humans

---

2. See "Emoticons" on page 59 for explanation of this symbol.

have been developing substitutes for live interaction since the invention of smoke signals.

The valid point in that statement is that electronic communication can't—and shouldn't—*completely* replace live human interaction. A case in point: The *Wall Street Journal*[3] reports on a group of managers who agreed to start using email less. Why? They found that because they solved most of their easy problems via email, they only met when they had to deal with something really nasty, which led to very unpleasant meetings. They agreed to meet more regularly (although still less frequently than they did before the advent of email) so as to stay on better terms with each other.

Email can be a great tool for dealing with people you can't stand in person. I once had to work with an incredibly nervous man whose tension was contagious. Rather than having him call me up at all hours of the day, we agreed to communicate by email. I sent him a project update every day or so, and if I left any of his questions unanswered, he would ask them by return email. I would try to reply by the end of the next day. I also tried to send him my reports right before I went home in the evening, so that if he did decide to follow up with a phone call, I'd be gone. It worked pretty well.

We still had to meet in person once in a while, though. You can't have everything.

Email Never-Neverland: home of the lost messages

Somewhere in cyberspace, there's a limbo of lost email messages. Like the souls of unbaptized babies, these notes wait, unread, for the end of time.

The Post Office has always had its dead letter office. Mail delivery in cyberspace is no more foolproof. The advantage of electronic delivery is that lost information isn't irretrievable; you usually have a copy of anything you sent to someone else.

---

3. *Wall Street Journal*, November 29, 1993, "Manager's Journal: Robert's Electronic Rules of Order" by Michael Schrage.

Sometimes the mail system will send you notification that your mail could not be delivered. When that happens, don't just resend the note; try to find out what the problem was. You may have put the wrong address on the message, or a gateway between mail systems might be down, or the other person's mail system might be down, or there might be a problem with your own mail system. Here's what to do:

- Ask around and find out whether your colleagues are having problems with your local mail system. If the answer is no,

- Call the other person and check whether you used the right email address.

- If you used the correct address, ask whether they've been having email problems.

If it turns out that you used the wrong address, you can just resend the message using the right one. If there's a mail system problem, or if you can't figure out what the problem is, you'll have to resend the message later or figure out alternative means of transferring the information.

If you're sending email to the Internet, and you don't have any other way of getting through, you can send a query to postmaster@yourrecipients.domain. Internet system administration convention requires that there be a real live person at the postmaster address, one who may or may not be willing to help with your problem. (Of course, this only works if you have the right domain name.)

If you've sent email to someone and haven't received a response as quickly as you expected, don't just assume that your correspondent is goofing off. Give him the benefit of the doubt and check whether your message ever arrived. This is a variation on the old grandparents' trick for eliciting prompt thank-you notes: "I didn't get a letter so I was worried that you didn't receive my gift." It works pretty well. If the note was, in fact, lost, you've done your correspondent a favor. And if it wasn't, you'll probably embarrass him into action.

5. *The Elements of Electronic Style*

The truth is that computer networking is still in its infancy. Probably nothing illustrates this more clearly than the "ASCII jail": 90% of network communications are still limited to plain old ASCII text—that is, the characters of the alphabet, the numerals 0 through 9, and the most basic punctuation marks. It's bad enough that multimedia communications have not been implemented in most of cyberspace. Most of the time you can't even put a word in bold or italics!

Because people cannot see or hear you in cyberspace, you need to pay close attention to the style of your electronic communications if you hope to make a good impression there. The *style* of electronic communications encompasses everything about your correspondence except its content, from your use of network conventions like "smileys" and "sigs" to the number of characters per line in your email messages.

Style considerations are influenced by several of the rules of Netiquette, especially Rule 4, Respect other people's time, and Rule 5, Make yourself look good online. It doesn't matter how brilliant your messages are if they're formatted in such a way that no one can read them.

Tone of voice online

The fact that most network interactions are limited to written words can be the source of misunderstandings. Fortunately, clever network users have had years to deal with this. They've created a shorthand to help communicate the tone that you'd otherwise get from the other person's voice, facial expressions, and gestures. These shorthand expressions are known as smileys or emoticons. They're easy to figure out once you get the hang of it. Just remember that they're all sideways faces.

See Table 1 for a list of the most commonly used emoticons. There are whole books about smileys for those who are interested, including the enjoyable *Smiley Dictionary* by Seth Godin.

People also use abbreviations to express emotional states or to qualify what they're saying. See Table 2 for a list of common abbreviations.

The "FLAME ON/FLAME OFF" notifier

When you really want to run off at the keyboard—but you want your readers to know that you know that you're not expressing yourself in your usual measured, reasoned manner—you need to let them know that you know that you're flaming. So before you begin your rant, simply enter the words FLAME ON. Then rant away. When you're done, write FLAME OFF and resume normal discourse. See "The Art of Flaming" on page 71 for more details.

Looking good online

One of the neat things about computers is that they let us use all kinds of special effects in our documents that we didn't even dream of back in the days of typewriters (if you're old enough to remember those days). But when you're communicating online, in most cases it's back to the typewriter as far as effects go. Even if your mail system lets you use boldface, italics, and tabs, there's no guarantee that your correspondent's system will understand them. At worst, your communication will turn into unreadable gibberish.

Table 1: Emoticons

:-)	Smile; laugh; "I'm joking"
:-(	Frown; sadness; "Bummer"
:)	Variant of :-) or "Have a nice day"
:(	Variant of :-(
;-)	Wink; denotes a pun or sly joke
:-O	Yelling or screaming; or completely shocked
:-()	Can't (or won't) stop talking
:-D	Big, delighted grin
:-P	Sticking out your tongue
:-] or :-}	Sarcastic smile
%-)	Confused but happy; drunk or under the influence of controlled substances
%-(	Confused and unhappy
:'-(	Crying
:'-)	Crying happy tears
:-|	Can't decide how to feel; no feelings either way
:-\	Mixed but mostly happy
:-/	Mixed but mostly sad
*	Kiss
{} or []	Hug
{{{***}}}	Hugs and kisses

Table 2: Abbreviations

BTW	By the way
IMHO	In my humble opinion
IMNSHO	In my not so humble opinion
IOW	In other words
IRL	In real life
ITRW	In the real world
LOL	Laughing out loud
MorF?	Male or Female? (used in chat areas for people with gender-neutral handles)
OTF	On the floor (laughing)
ROTFL	Rolling on the floor laughing
RTFM	Read the f***ing manual (said in response to a stupid question)
WRT	With regard to
YMMV	Your mileage may vary
<g> or <G>	Grin
<bg>	Big grin

What to do?

- Forget about boldface, italics, tabs, and font changes. Never use any effect you couldn't get on an old-fashioned typewriter. In fact, you can't even use all of those. Underlining won't work, for example. Nor can you use the old "required backspace" trick to put a diacritical mark (a tilde or an accent mark, for example) over another character.

- Most systems won't read the diacritical marks anyway, so just leave them out. If you feel an accent mark is absolutely necessary, type an apostrophe *after* the letter the accent would have gone over.

- Use only ASCII characters. This includes all 26 letters of the alphabet (upper and lower case), the numerals 0 through 9, and most commonly used punctuation marks. For any publishing mavens out there, however, it excludes em dashes ("—"), en dashes ("–"), and bullets.

- Limit your line length to 80 characters, or better yet,

  60 characters.

  Otherwise, your lines may break in weird places and

  your readers

  will have to wade through notes that look like this.

  Believe me,

  it gets annoying after a very short while.

- NEVER TYPE YOUR NOTES IN ALL CAPS, LIKE THIS. It's rude—like shouting constantly. And, like constant shouting, it makes people stop listening. All caps may be used, IN MODERA-TION, for emphasis.

- To indicate *italics,* you may *surround the material to be italicized with asterisks.*

- To indicate <u>underlining</u>, surround the material with _underscores_. Use this for book references as well—for example, this book is called _Netiquette_.

Signature files

Some systems allow people to create a "signature file" or "sig file." These signatures automatically appear at the end of each message the person sends. They usually contain the person's full name and often include cute quotes or little drawings. For example:

```
    A\    Seth Ross
   A A\    Publisher, Albion Books
  A    A\   4547 California St., San Francisco, CA 94118
 AAAAAAA\   seth@albion.com, 415-752-7666, fax 415-752-5417
A        A\  "Computer books for a converging world."
```

Some people rant about oversized or silly signatures. But from a time-wasting point of view, they're not really that big a deal. Since they're automatically inserted at the end of the message, you can read the whole message without looking at the whole sig. On the other hand, the force of human curiosity that drives us onto the net in the first place makes it hard for many of us to ignore screens full of type, even if we know there's probably nothing worth reading there.

One positive aspect of sigs is that they often contain "offline" contact information. This can actually save time and bandwidth because it allows people to respond privately by telephone or by (gasp) U.S. mail. By placing an email address in a sig, the sender is also hedging against the chance that the email "header" message may get garbled in transit.

In most situations, Netiquette frowns on excessive sigs and smiles on pithy ones. Keep in mind that some public access Internet sites automatically restrict sigs to four lines. Silly sigs are definitely not recommended for business correspondence—see "Electronic Mail at Work" on page 91 for a discussion of the rules of business email.

Bottom line: Excessively long signatures are a waste of bandwidth. So it couldn't hurt to keep your signature file down to, say, six lines max, four lines preferred.

6. *Netiquette for Discussion Groups*

You and your virtual buddies

Much of your cyberspace interaction will take place in discussion groups—areas where notes on a topic of common interest are posted and stored for anyone to read. Discussion groups are also known as newsgroups, message boards, bulletin boards, and forums. To participate, you read the notes that people have posted over the last few days. You write your own response and post it yourself. Then you check in the next day and see how other people responded to you.

When you first start posting messages to discussion groups, you may feel shy. That's good—it's a sign that you're concerned about the impression you're going to make on a bunch of people you've never met. Fortunately, most discussion group readers are there in the first place because they're friendly people who enjoy interacting with others. (Although there's a very loud minority that takes pleasure in tearing down other people and their ideas; see "The Art of Flaming" on page 71 for more.) Here are some hints on making friends, not enemies, in cyberspace:

- If you're getting started with USENET newsgroups, check out the many useful articles in the news.announce.newusers and news.-newusers.questions newsgroups. Do this before you post anything anywhere.

- Lurk for a while before you post. "Lurking" is reading the discussion group correspondence without actually participating. Don't worry; despite the sinister tone of the word, lurking in cyberspace is not frowned upon—in fact, it's encouraged. Lurking gives you an idea of who the participants are and what the tone of the discussion is. It helps you avoid mistaking a joke for a serious statement, or posting a comment only to find out that a virtually identical statement appeared in the group yesterday.

- Get and read a copy of the FAQ (Frequently Asked Questions) document for the group, if it has one. FAQs are incredibly useful documents, often containing more information than many basic textbooks. (They're better written than most textbooks, too.) The FAQ will give you a base level of knowledge that most of the other people in the discussion group share. You can get the FAQs for many USENET newsgroups by anonymous FTP from the Internet site rtfm.mit.edu.

- When you start posting, post appropriate comments and questions. Try to fit in with the tone and style of the discussion group. That doesn't mean you should erase the few traces of individuality that remain to you after years of formal schooling. Just behave like a participant in a constructive discussion.

- Make sure you're in the right newsgroup. If you think that Barney the dinosaur is the best thing to happen to children's TV since Kermit the frog, don't waste your time in the USENET newsgroup alt.barney.dinosaur.die.die.die. And don't post notes saying "I HATE CATS" to rec.pets.cats. Nobody there cares.

- When someone writes something that makes you mad (and someone will), resist the impulse to flame back. One angry response can beget a long and destructive flame war.

- Phrase your postings politely. Cursing is frowned upon (except in designated areas like the USENET newsgroup alt.tasteless). If you want to express a strong opinion, cute euphemisms and made-up expletives are usually acceptable.

- Make sure your postings are correct. This is particularly important with information about serious topics—for example, an illness. Information—whether true or false—spreads rapidly through cyberspace. You wouldn't want to be responsible for making people sicker than they already were.

- Don't assume that posted information is correct, and don't spread it around if you have any questions at all about it.

- Be careful about posting late at night or any time you're tired, sick, or having a terrible day. Your judgment may not be at its best. When in doubt, hold off until you feel better.

Developing time-saving habits

Many of the basic Netiquette rules for discussion groups fall under Rule 4, Respect other people's time. Here they are:

- When posting to a discussion group, try not to ask stupid questions. I'm familiar with the belief that "there's no such thing as a stupid question." On the net, that's not necessarily the case. A stupid question is one that you could have found the answer to yourself with a little research, or one that you're asking in the wrong place. If you do the basic research suggested here (i.e., read the FAQ) and don't find the answer to your question, and you have reason to believe that you're looking for the answer in the right place, go ahead and ask. Fortunately, most network surfers are kindly folks who will be happy to help you out, even if your question is considered stupid. But it's only polite not to take advantage of their time if you don't have to. So read the FAQ. If your question is answered there, you didn't waste anyone's time either reading or answering it.

- If the FAQ doesn't answer your question, go ahead and post. But, if you still suspect that it's a request for some fairly basic information, ask that responses be sent to you by email. That way, you're not responsible for discussion group readers having to wade through screens full of identical answers.

- Use descriptive and specific subject lines. This helps others decide whether your particular words of wisdom relate to a topic they care about.

- Try not to post comments that don't add anything to the discussion. When you're just cruising through a thread in a leisurely manner, it's not too annoying to read through a lot of "hear, hear"'s and "I agree"'s. But if you're actually trying to find information, it's a pain in the neck. So save those one-word responses for threads that have degenerated to the point where none but true aficionados are following them any more.

- If your posting is only of interest to a specific geographic area, try to limit the distribution to that area. I live in California; even if I wanted to, I couldn't easily adopt a cat that lives in Boston.

- Post messages to the appropriate discussion group. It may seem obvious, but don't post stories or questions about fighter planes to a newsgroup for gardeners. If you're in doubt, it's always OK to ask—but ask briefly. I once read a long (and apparently sincere) posting in a discussion group for feminists from a guy who was looking for tips on how to meet women. He did have the sense to acknowledge that this might not be the best place to start his search. But he should have stopped there and asked for confirmation and suggestions for other groups to ask.

Things never to post to a discussion group

- Requests to have your name added to a mailing list. There is *always* a separate email address for such requests; for Internet and BITNET lists, it usually starts with "LISTSERV" or "listname-request." Find it and use it.

- Requests for the FAQ. These can usually be obtained from a "LISTSERV" address as well.

- Answers to basic or stupid questions. If you feel charitable enough to send an answer, send it by email directly to the asker; don't burden the entire readership with it. This goes for any question you think will get a lot of identical responses.

Q. How do I handle it when new or careless users waste our time by sending test messages or requests to be added to the list to the discussion group?

First, assume that they are new, not careless—that they simply don't know any better. Then, politely and sympathetically inform them of their error *by email.* Don't post your correction to the group. Say something like, "You must not have realized that there is a newsgroup just for test messages. If you use it, you won't interrupt the readers of rec.tv.wonder-years" or "FYI, here's how to sign up for a mailing list. This way, only the system administrator gets your request—not everyone on the list. Welcome to the group!" Be friendly about it.

As a rule, don't post this note to the discussion group—that's usually a prescription for a really stupid flame war. If several people post inappropriate messages within a few days, it may be a sign that a fresh boatload of newbies has arrived in your area. In that case, go ahead and post an explanation of proper posting behavior—but again, say it nicely.

7. *The Art of Flaming*

Although flames often get out of hand, they have a purpose in the ecology of cyberspace. Many flames are aimed at teaching someone something (usually in overstated language) or stopping them from doing something (like offending other people). Flame messages often use more brute force than is strictly necessary, but that's half the fun.

Netiquette does ask that you consider the *art* of flaming before pulling out the flame-thrower. Any wannabe with an email account can ignite a firestorm of ill-conceived and boring flames. It takes diligence and creativity to pull off an artful flame. Who knows—if your flame is good enough, you might even make it into the Hall of Flame (see "Flame newsgroups" on page 79).

Choose your flames well

If you must flame, don't flame gratuitously. Choose your target with care. In other words, hold back on flaming the newcomer to a discussion group who asks a dumb question. Or the prophet of doom who posts his "the end is near" message to the entire USENET newsgroup hierarchy.[4] In addition, think twice before flaming the gurus on the net. This won't earn you popularity points and, most likely, the guru will

---

4. Someone actually did this in the aftermath of the 1994 LA earthquake. The net responded with reams of flameage, an utter waste of time.

have the last word. Remember that a poorly executed flame is worse than no flame at all.

Know your facts before you start flaming

Any time you flame you're going out on a limb. Check your facts. Check your spelling. Check your citations if you've quoted someone else. Check that you're sending it to the right group. Submit the flame to a sanity check, remembering that the net never forgets.

Use FLAME ON/FLAME OFF markers

It's good form to warn readers that you're about to let off steam. Just write "FLAME ON" at the beginning of a diatribe to let readers know what's coming. That way, they may still be offended, but at least they were warned. Additionally, the "FLAME ON" marker can indicate that you yourself don't take the diatribe entirely seriously. When you've finished flaming, write "FLAME OFF" and resume normal discourse.

Don't respond to flame-bait

Flame-bait is a public statement deliberately designed to provoke flames. Usually those who post flame-bait are looking for attention. You're best off not giving it.

Avoid needless escalation

One sure way to escalate a flame war is to expand the battleground. This can be accomplished by carbon copying the world on your flames or by cross-posting your flame to other discussion groups. There's nothing worse than an escalating flame war that barges into the middle of a civil discussion. Usually the innocent readers didn't witness the beginning of the war and thus don't have the context necessary to pick the winner. The skillful flamer keeps the heat in the proper place and avoids needless escalation.

Flame wars

The USENET news group rec.food.veg is famous for its flame wars. One favorite of mine was about whether vegans or omnivores were more subject to vitamin B-12 deficiencies. It got pretty ugly.

Flame wars can be amusing for the twisted among us to read. (I particularly enjoy reading the outrageous flames sent by readers complaining about the flame wars.) Nevertheless, it's generally considered rude to subject other readers in a discussion group to a protracted flame war, especially when it gets personal. Perhaps more important, prolonged participation in a flame war can get you a really bad reputation on a discussion group. Imagine losing the respect of hundreds—even thousands—of people you've never even met! If you want that kind of abuse, you might as well run for president; the pay is better if you win.

USENET participant Graham Wolff Christian points out that flame wars are almost ubiquitous. He writes

```
*Every* discussion list of which I have been a
part--no matter what its subject--has fallen
victim to such ills--a few have gone down in
e-flames. The pattern is absolutely consis-
tent. Writer A drops a light remark--always
*tangential* to the main discussion. Writer B
interprets the message in the worst possible
light and fires off an outraged reply, in which
writer A is called a racist, a classist, a fas-
cist--whatever seems to apply. Writers C-L
chime in, rather like the crowds in a DeMille
film, muttering "Shame!" or "I agree!" or "A
is right!" or "B is right!" Writer A replies
saying, "Gosh, it was just a joke. I'm not a
fascist. Lighten up." Writer B says, "This is-
sue (the South, date rape, Nicaragua) is DEAD-
LY SERIOUS. I won't lighten up. I won't." By
the time things have cooled down, Writers A and
B have left the list; or Writers N-DD have left
the list; or the list has died. These are not
*odd* occasions--they happen to *every list.*
```

In the worst-case scenario, a protracted flame war can destroy a discussion group. Inevitably, the least common denominator principle takes hold, and the group sinks to the level of the loudest and lowest flamers.

The problem flamer

Although flaming isn't necessarily bad Netiquette, a flamer can sometimes get out of hand. For example, say you participate in the ultra-
friendly newsgroup rec.pets.cats. Somebody posts a message to the
newsgroup suggesting that all kittens should be "buried up to their
necks at lawn-mowing time." What do you do?

Your first impulse may be to respond to the culprit—either publicly or
by private email—casting aspersions on his/her morals, intelligence,
ancestry, etc. Don't do it. People who post flagrantly offensive flames
like this are either flexing their net.muscles, or desperately crying out
for attention, or some combination of those things. Many (perhaps
most) such flamers are college students who have just discovered
cyberspace, and whose social skills haven't yet caught up with their
technical abilities. A return flame may be just what they want, and in
any case probably won't change their behavior.

Some better suggestions (offered by the friendly folks on rec.-
pets.cats):[5]

1. Ask your moderator to stop posting anything the flamer writes.
   (This isn't an option on an unmoderated newsgroup like rec.-
   pets.cats. If there were a moderator, the offensive posting probably
   would never have appeared.)

2. On the theory that attention is what the flamer wants, just ignore
   him/her.

3. Use your news reader's "kill file" feature to prevent anything the
   flamer writes from appearing on your screen.

4. In cases of flagrant abuse, you can try sending a note to the flamer's
   system administrator asking for him/her to intervene. But save this
   for extreme cases of repeated, abusive postings. Don't waste the

---

5. Thanks to Desiree McCrorey, Jim Graham, Kay Klier, David Wren-Hardin, and
others on rec.pets.cats.

sysadmin's time just because someone on his/her system was having a bad day.

5. Send a chilly note to the miscreant. Kay Klier's version is "Your post to rec.pets.cats was inappropriate to this news group. Please do not post similar material here again." Kay often receives an apologetic reply to this note. Other times, the flamer simply disappears from the newsgroup. Occasionally, someone will reply abusively. If that happens, you can forward the reply to the writer's system administrator and ask to have the person gently reminded of proper network behavior.

Netiquette recommends solution 5 for several reasons:

- It always feels better to take action.

- As world events demonstrate, ignoring those who are childishly screaming for attention doesn't always make them stop. Better to gently point out the error of their ways; at least you tried.

The varieties of flaming experience

Flames tend to proceed along predictable patterns. That is, the same flames are repeated over and over again in different forums and at different times. Below are some classic flames.

The Spelling Flame

It happens every day. Someone misspells a word in a public message. One or more people absolutely must publicly correct the error. Judging from the number of times this happens, there seem to be millions of high school English teacher wannabes in cyberspace. Ironically, spelling flames nearly always contain spelling errors.

Spelling flames are bad Netiquette. If you feel absolutely compelled to correct someone's spelling or grammar, do so via private email. Keep in mind that English is not the first language of many people on the Internet.

If you receive such a flame, ignore it publicly, thank the sender privately, or gently remind him of the destructiveness of such flames.

The Grammar Flame

A close relative of the spelling flame, grammar flames can be even more treacherous because the rules of grammar are less clearly defined than spelling. Avoid flaming for grammar.

The Bandwidth Flame

The Bandwidth Flame category covers a lot of ground, including flames about posting to the wrong group, posting too many messages to a group, or posting stupid messages. This one usually starts, "Do you know how many gadzillions of people had to read your useless message?" When you issue a Bandwidth Flame, you're actually wasting bandwidth. Such flames should be taken to private email, particularly if the bandwidth waster is a newcomer. Some people are persistent time-wasters: sometimes the only way to make them stop is to turn up the heat publicly. But usually, your Bandwidth Flame will invite a flaming response.

One reason Bandwidth Flames are so common is that people access cyberspace in a variety of ways. Some people are sitting at the end of high-bandwidth T1 links to the net paid for by their employer. Others sit at the end of 2400-baud modem connections that they pay for by the minute. If you have a high-bandwidth connection, be considerate of those who don't. If you have a pay-per-minute connection, don't be surprised when an awful lot of messages seem wasteful.

The Clueless Newbie Flame

This flame results from disparities of knowledge and experience. The clueless newbie stumbles into a discussion group and starts posting stupid questions. Old timers and wizards then flame at will. This is a cheap flame. It's just too easy. All cybernauts begin as newbies. If you're an experienced net citizen, remember that you were a newbie at one point in your net career.

If you're a clueless newbie yourself, check the next flame closely.

The RTFM Flame

Read the f***ing manual. Do it. Don't post stupid questions before consulting the FAQ or manual. Of course, in some cases there is no manual (in which case there's no excuse for an RTFM Flame). In others, the manual might not answer your question.

If you go blundering around the net posting the first question that comes to mind in forum after forum, expect RTFM flameage. To the extent that this kind of flame encourages people to solve their own problems, it has salutary effects. A good way to handle those who persist in refusing to RTFM is to politely refer them to the correct manual or FAQ. An exact page or paragraph reference adds an amusing tone of condescension.

The My-Computer-Is-Better-Than-Yours Flame

Judging from billions of "my computer is better than yours" messages, many people really love their computers. This a sure-fire flame war starter. Go ahead: log into Macintosh forum and start posting about how much greater your PC is than any Mac. Before the flame war has run its course, someone's bound to chime in about all the wonderful features of the Amiga that Mac and PC users miss.

"Advocacy" discussions that compare the features of different computers or operating systems can be informative. They also get old quite quickly. If you feel the need to discuss the relative merits of different technologies, consider posting to one of the many "advocacy" newsgroups featured in USENET's "comp" hierarchy (i.e., comp.sys.mac.advocacy, comp.sys.next.advocacy etc.).

The Get-a-Life Flame

Some people hang out in cyberspace to the exclusion of real life activities. It's not good Netiquette to tell them to "get a life." People who tell others to get a life probably don't have one themselves. If you're on the receiving end of this kind of flame, grin and bear it. A reply with evidence that you do have a life is unlikely to be effective.

The PC Flame

This flame can crop up practically anywhere. The classic formula: someone makes a sexist/racist/homophobic/fascist remark, and a hundred watchdogs step in and flame at will.

Those with evolved sensibilities bear special responsibilities here. We must realize that not everyone is as enlightened as we are. The chance that you'll change the mind or heart of an ignoramus via a flame is negligible. In fact, your flameage may be exactly what the sexist/racist, etc. lout wants in the first place. If you're a sensitive person, it may be best to avoid the many hang-outs of the politically incorrect.

On the other hand, Netiquette doesn't require you to stand idly by while other people spout offensive nonsense. Answer as passionately and forcibly as you like, but avoid personal attacks. A calm, logical response always strengthens your position. Listening to what the other person is trying to say doesn't hurt either.

The Advertising Flame

The Advertising Flame is an Internet classic. Given the Internet's research and educational missions, it's not surprising that overt commercial advertising traditionally has been frowned upon by Internet culture. For years, the NSF's Acceptable Use Policy (AUP) has flatly forbidden use of the NSFNET backbone for commercial purposes. This stricture is often ignored, in part because it's unenforceable. Even sites where the AUP is in effect allow "informational" postings about new products that read like advertising, are written by ad copywriters, and often contain prices and ordering information.[6]

Now, the commercialization of the Internet is in full swing. Thousands of businesses have connected to the Internet in the past few years, bringing with them a more tolerant business climate. Barriers to commercialization will be lifted as the net progresses. Nonetheless, overtly

---

6. If you're looking for legitimate places to adver...I mean, post product information, check out the USENET "biz" hierarchy, comp.newproducts, and various "*.forsale" groups.

commercial messages will always be flame-bait in many parts of cyber-space. After all, no one wants to be bombarded with commercial messages or see the net turn into a nausea-provoking advertising machine like Prodigy.

If you post new product announcements, self-promotions, or ad copy where it's not expressly allowed, be prepared for flameage. Unsolicited direct email advertising is probably the worse transgression. Consider this: in conventional direct mail, a 2% response rate is considered decent. If your company experiments with unsolicited direct email, don't be surprised if you get a 98% response, from people flaming you for clogging up their electronic mailboxes.

The Gross-Out Flame

Otherwise known as the Deliberately Offensive Flame. By definition, these flames have no redeeming value. Often they involve uncalled for personal attacks. Sometimes they amount to no more than racist or sexist drivel (see "The PC Flame" on page 78). Netiquette forbids gross-out flames, except in clearly marked gross-out domains (see "Flame newsgroups" below).

"Censorship" on the net

One of the remedies noted above for errant flamers is appealing to the culprit's sysadmin or to the newsgroup moderator to have network privileges revoked. This will no doubt elicit cries of "censorship!" from some. Sorry. Currently, no network service that I'm aware of is run as a democracy. While scorn is rightly heaped on such services as Prodigy—which monitor discussion group content ruthlessly for anything that could be construed as remotely offensive—there is such a thing as Going Too Far in almost any group. Privately owned and managed groups do have a right to monitor and censor their contents.

Flame newsgroups

Some USENET newsgroups, like alt.flame and alt.tasteless, exist purely for the purpose of sharing rude and offensive writings. There's even a "Hall of Flame" newsgroup: alt.flame.hall-of-flame. Surprisingly, even these groups have their own etiquette, but it's frequently breached, and there's not much you can do about it. If you're having a really bad day, you might try posting to alt.flame; at least you never have to worry about negative repercussions. One of my own favorites is alt.flame.roommate. If you have roommates, you'll empathize; if you don't—and especially if you used to and don't any more—it'll remind you how lucky you are.

Apologizing

Q. I sent flame mail to a discussion group I participate in, and now I regret it. What should I do?

A gracious apology is almost always appreciated. Here's a good example of one:

```
>>Sorry for the flame yesterday. Bad day. I too
appreciate a flame-free environment.<<
```

Note that this method can be used to retract or to correct statements you made, or simply to apologize for the manner in which you spoke. You can stand by what you said but regret the way you said it. Like calling a flamer on his actions, this takes some courage. But most readers will appreciate the effort and remove you from their scum-of-the-earth lists.

8. *Netiquette for Information Retrieval*

When you retrieve information across the net, you're not interacting directly with other humans. So Netiquette for this activity is fairly simple, and is mostly governed by Rule 4, Don't waste other people's time and bandwidth.

Although time and bandwidth are different—bandwidth is information-carrying capacity; time is time—in practice, conserving one tends to conserve the other. Conserving bandwidth is particularly important when you retrieve information from a host or server, because carelessness about your own usage can prevent other people from getting information they need. Only a limited number of people can be connected to a server at any one time. And a server can only transmit a certain amount of information per second. When too many people are trying to download too much information, some users are denied access, and system performance slows down for everyone.

What can you do to prevent that? Here are some simple rules:

* Don't stay logged in when you're not doing anything.

* If possible, log in at off-peak hours.

- Connect to hosts that are geographically nearby.[7] I know it's more fun to connect with the University of Freiburg than with the college across town, but local connections put less strain on the Internet backbone.

- Download only files you actually need.

- If a file looks interesting but you're not entirely sure what it is, download and read the associated README file. The README file is usually short, and is always a simple text file, so downloading it won't use a lot of time or bandwidth. Once you read it, you'll be able to decide whether to download the file itself.

---

7. Remember:
A host is a host
From coast to coast
But always connect to the host that's close.

9. *Egregious Violations of Netiquette*

Just like the real world, cyberspace contains people who commit flagrant acts of misbehavior. Fortunately, these people are in the minority. Unfortunately, we have to watch out for them anyway. Here are a few egregious violations of Netiquette to be on the alert for as you travel through cyberspace.

Cyberspace predators

Perhaps the worst Netiquette violators are people who use their cyberspace connections to gain the trust of others and then take advantage of them in real life. Some of the most unpleasant stories involve pedophiles who get to know kids online, engage in sexual discussions with them, and in some cases, arrange to meet them live.

Children aren't the only ones who are vulnerable to this kind of abuse. The story of the "Net Lothario" (page 117) is an example of how adults can also be fooled by someone who lacks morals and writes persuasively.

This doesn't mean that you can't trust anyone you meet online. It does mean that you need to exercise at least as much caution with your cyberspace acquaintances as you would with a friendly person you met at the grocery store. In fact, because it's so easy for predators to misrepresent themselves online, a little more caution is in order.

Children, in particular, should be warned never to give out personal information—their addresses, their phone numbers, their passwords, or the times they're home alone—online. And unfortunately, every cybernaut needs to remember that fellow net travelers may not be who or what they claim to be.

Alternate personae

Many people who create false identities online aren't predators—they're just fooling around. In many areas of cyberspace—particularly MUDs (multi-user dungeons) and their close cousins, MOOs (object-oriented MUDs)—it's normal and expected behavior. MUDs and MOOs exist specifically for the purpose of exploring fantasy worlds and fantasy identities. Men often represent themselves as women. (For some reason, it's less common for women to appear as men.) All that is just fine.

Other cases are closer to the borderline of acceptable behavior. For instance, male journalists have created feminine handles to investigate sexual harassment on the net. While that isn't particularly nice, neither is sexual harassment. Netiquette permits it as long as the journalist refrains from getting deeply involved with anyone under false pretenses. The story of "Joan" (page 118) is an example of a man whose "experiment" in cyberspace cross-dressing got out of control.

Long-term misrepresentation of oneself in romance discussion groups or chat areas, where the purpose of the interaction is to form a serious relationship, is definitely not acceptable. See "Love & Sex in Cyberspace" on page 115 for details.

Electronic forgery

Every piece of email and every posting to a discussion group carries an electronic signature. And, just as it's possible to forge a handwritten signature, it is sometimes possible to send email from someone else's ID. A recent example occurred when five college freshmen decided it would be funny to send a false letter of resignation for a new university official. They also circulated demands for tuition to other students and letters implying that the official was gay. Administrators had begun acting on the resignation before they found out it was a fake.

In another bizarre incident, readers of alt.fan.douglas-adams, the USENET fan club for *Hitchhiker's Guide to the Galaxy* author Douglas Adams, started circulating rumors that genuine postings from Adams—who occasionally reads the newsgroup—were fake. Then an actual fake Douglas Adams started sending abusive notes to readers. The real Douglas Adams had a terrible time straightening out the mess.

Forging email is just as wrong as forging a paper letter. Forged email is also fairly easy to trace. Bad idea.

Chain letters

Have you ever gotten one of those letters promising you millions of dollars if you just send a few dollars to a list of people, but threatening you with hideous death within a year if you don't? Those things circulate in cyberspace as well. The best-known is a long, rambling letter signed by "Dave Rhodes." It appears periodically in random discussion groups and mailboxes.

Chain letters are forbidden on BITNET and on most commercial network services. If you receive a copy of the "Dave Rhodes" letter, or any other chain letter, don't follow the instructions! Forward a copy to your system administrator or postmaster and request that action be taken against the sender. You can also reply to the sender yourself and tell him or her that sending chain letters is not acceptable network behavior.

Electronic hoaxes

Some people don't stop with forging email from real people. Some people construct entire fictional companies and publicize them on the net.

A recent example that received a lot of publicity was the Sexonix hoax. A fellow named Joey Skaggs announced to the media that he had set up the world's first virtual reality sex provider, called "Sexonix." He actually rented a booth at a Canadian trade show to show off his wares. Then he claimed that the Canadian government had seized all of his hardware and software on his way to the show. He posted a press release to The WELL claiming that the seizure had destroyed his business. The trouble was, he had no hardware, no software, and no business except that of fooling people.

In this case, the worst thing that happened was probably that the people who were fooled felt—well, foolish. But it's not hard to imagine stories that could have far more dangerous consequences. Hoaxes are bad Netiquette.

Rumors

A close cousin to the hoax is the rumor. Two rumors that weren't invented maliciously have gained special prominence on the net. The first is the Craig Shergold story. Here's the true part: A number of years ago, Craig Shergold, a young English boy, was diagnosed with an inoperable brain tumor. He decided that before he died, he wanted to make it into the *Guinness Book of World Records* for receiving the most get-well cards ever. He succeeded. Better yet, a wealthy American had the idea that maybe Craig's cancer wasn't inoperable. He paid for Craig to see specialists in America. It turned out that the type of cancer had been misdiagnosed, the tumor was removed, and when last heard from, Craig was fine.

Well, almost fine. Somewhere along the way, Craig's request for get-well cards mutated into a request for business cards. And the news that Craig was fine didn't spread as fast as the requests. Craig's mailbox has been piled full of unwanted business cards for three or four years now. It's driving his mother crazy! If you see this story, *please* tell the well-intentioned person who passed it on that the cards are no longer wanted and Craig is well.

The other rumor that resurfaces periodically is the modem tax story. Several years ago, the U.S. Congress did discuss imposing a special "telecommunications tax" on modems. A call to action was posted and protests were lodged. Eventually, the idea was dropped. Unfortunately, the call to action posting wasn't. If you see this story floating around, squelch it immediately.

Email harassment

It's hard to believe, but some people are both stupid and venal enough to harass their colleagues via email. I know of one case in which a male manager started emailing outrageous sexual suggestions to a female employee. Initially, the notes were fairly innocuous—for example, "That was a great-looking dress you had on yesterday." Over time, they progressed into obscenity. The really funny part was that about half of each note would be more or less pornographic, and the other half would be perfectly reasonable business correspondence.

The employee, being far smarter than her boss, simply saved copies of the notes. When the situation got out of control, she took them to the human resources department. Everything she needed to prove her case was right there, including the dates and times the messages were sent. Her manager, of course, was fired.

With a milder form of harassment—for example, Joe Schmoe keeps sending the blonde joke of the day to everyone in the department—less drastic steps might be in order. If you don't object to other people reading blonde jokes but don't want to get them yourself, send a reply to one of Joe's messages and ask him to take you off his mailing list. If you feel that his use of company resources is inappropriate and should be stopped, tell him so. But in either case, keep copies of everything. If the situation ever escalates, you'll have backup.

Worms and viruses

Right up there with the email harassers and the rumor-mongers are the people who get kicks out of sending worms and viruses throughout cyberspace. Cornell graduate student Robert Tappan Morris became notorious in 1988, when he shut down large areas of the Internet with a program—variously described as a worm or as a virus—that succeeded beyond his wildest dreams.

Morris actually intended this stunt as a harmless experiment; he had no intention of shutting down the Internet. He saw that there was a "back door" in the Internet email system and wanted to see how far he could go with it. He found out—and paid for it with a federal conviction for "computer fraud."

Morris made a big mistake. There's no excuse for repeating it.

Snooping

Various types of networks can make it more or less easy to get into another person's personal files. On Macintosh networks, it's possible to publish your entire hard disk as a server, making all your files accessible to anyone on the network.

Even if you should happen by a machine that—essentially—has its front door wide open, don't snoop. You're not in the habit of walking up to people's houses and trying their front doors, are you? (I hope not!)

If, because of your position or your superior knowledge, you have the power to snoop in other people's mail or files, it's even more important that you don't do it. It can be very tempting. But their mail is really none of your business. Netiquette forbids the abuse of power (see "Rule 9: Don't abuse your power" on page 44).

Keep in mind that Netiquette alone does not protect the privacy of your email. See "Email Privacy—A Grand Illusion?" on page 125.

Mailbombing

Sometimes, annoyed discussion group readers will try to take vengeance on a particularly obnoxious flamer by flooding his mailbox. This is called mailbombing, and it's a bad idea. Yes, it annoys the miscreant. But it also eats up hard disk space and wastes system administrator time for other users of that person's server. Don't do it.

Part III
Business Netiquette

10. *Electronic Mail at Work*

The conventions for email at work are a little different than for email among friends. Professional email can still be informal. But a lot of the humor and wit that's appropriate in a discussion group is out of place at work. For the most part, signature files are not used in work email, unless the email is sent to external recipients.

Q. My organization just installed an email system, and everyone is starting to use it. How often do I need to check my mail?

Preferably three or four times a day, but at least twice a day. You should always check your mail in the morning when you come in to the office and in mid-afternoon, or an hour or two before you leave. That way, you pick up messages that were sent while you were out of the office (late-evening messages if you're a morning person, early-morning messages if you're not) and act on them immediately. Your mid-afternoon check allows you to deal with the day's business promptly. A midday check and a final check before you leave for the day are always a good idea, as well.

If you're really too busy to check your mail that often, or if you're going to be out for more than a day, consider deputizing someone to check your mail. Giving out your password is generally not recommended. But you can put a temporary password on your mail system while you're away and change it back later. Some systems also allow you to set up a limited-access password for the person screening your mail.

Another useful feature, called "answermail" or "vacation" in the UNIX world, lets you write a message that automatically responds to anyone who sends you email while you're away. The message tells your correspondent how long you'll be gone and whom to contact if the information is urgent. This is a great feature; if you have it, use it. Do be careful, however, if you've subscribed to mailing lists. If the program automatically responds to everyone on the list, thousands of uninterested people could be forced to read about your vacation schedule.

The effects of email on the working world

If you've been working for more than a few years, you remember when electronic mail was quite unusual. Today it's commonplace, and it's changing the way we work. It can even affect us physically. I gained about 20 pounds in the two years after email was installed throughout my workplace, and I'm pretty sure it was because I had so much less running around to do. (It's a good excuse, anyway.)

Email has made a number of major changes in the way business functions:

- Since many executives read their own email, rather than having it screened like their paper mail and phone calls, it's often possible to contact powerful people directly.

- Many systems make it easy to send mail out to everyone at the site or everyone at the company.

- Email overload: Some people receive dozens of messages per day. Others don't actually receive that much mail, but can't seem to handle it anyway.

- Snail-mail ignorers: Other people get so used to doing everything over the wires that they forget—or don't bother—to read their paper mail.

Is all this good, bad, or indifferent? Probably some of all three. Let's handle each one of these issues in turn.

Emailing the CEO

A recent *New Yorker* article, entitled "E-mail from Bill," published the email address of Bill Gates, chairman of software giant Microsoft and one of the richest men in America.[1] In the article, Gates says (via email, of course), "I am the only person who reads my email so no one has to worry about embarrassing themselves or going around people when they send a message."

This is an interesting statement on a number of levels. First of all, Gates is making it clear that he doesn't mind getting email from the world—presumably (one hopes) he gave permission to the *New Yorker* to reprint his email address, something the magazine would never consider doing with, say, the direct dial phone line to his office. Second, he says that he doesn't need a secretary, assistant, or other gatekeeper to screen his messages. (This doesn't mean that he doesn't screen them himself; elsewhere in the same note he says, "If someone isn't saying something of interest, it's easier not to respond to their mail than it is not to answer the phone.")

But perhaps most interesting is the statement that "no one has to worry about embarrassing themselves" when they email him directly. I don't know about anyone else, but I'd worry a lot more about saying something stupid in email to Bill Gates than I would if I were talking on the phone to his secretary. Sure, his secretary might tell him I sounded like a jerk; but if I were nice enough, I'd probably get a positive report. And most of the managers I've known take their secretaries' character assessments very seriously.

---

1. "A Reporter at Large: E-Mail From Bill" by John Seabrook, in the *New Yorker*, Jan. 10, 1994.

The point is that when you introduce yourself via email, not only are you making a first impression, you're also leaving a written record. So use caution, especially when dealing with powerful people.

Additionally, not all chairmen and CEOs are as willing to receive information directly as Gates is. The fact that your company president's email address is listed in the organizational directory doesn't necessarily mean he wants to hear directly from his rank and file employees. And even if he doesn't mind, your own boss, or your boss's boss, might not be too pleased to learn that you circumvented his authority and went straight to the top. It depends on the politics of your organization.

Finally, some executives do have their secretaries screen their email. So if you do decide to send email directly to your company president—or to Bill Gates, for that matter—don't assume that he'll be the only person to read it. Bill may decide to hire an email screener now that his address is public knowledge.

Q. When should I give out another person's email address?

Anytime it would also be appropriate to give out a work phone number.

Emailing the company

A true story:

Two middle managers at a large computer company—both married to other people—were having an affair. They started sending each other pornographic love notes over the company email system. One day, one of them accidentally sent one of these missives to everyone at company headquarters. Both were fired.

The moral of this story is:

(a) Be faithful to your spouse.

(b) Don't cheat on your spouse on company time.

(c) Don't send anything over email that you wouldn't want published on the front page of *USA Today*.

(d) Delete the "all-at-company-headquarters" alias from your personal address list immediately.

I'll leave it to you to choose the moral that best suits your beliefs and lifestyle.

Here's another true story: An employee at a small company was severely allergic to perfumes and other fragrances. She sent flame mail to the entire organization demanding that everyone immediately cease using all scented products. The next day, someone sprayed perfume all over her office.

Note that Netiquette condones neither the flame mail nor the perfume-spraying. The point, however, is that the arrogance and rude tone of the mail provoked the extreme reaction. The fact that you have the capability to send mail instantaneously to large groups of people doesn't make it a good idea. Completely apart from the ethics of the situations described here, you need to be *really careful* if you have access to an all-company mailing list.

Some companies don't make it so easy for their employees to send mail to everyone in the organization. Where I used to work, one person (for awhile it was me) had to screen every message that was sent out to all employees. We needed to do that because our system didn't let users prioritize their messages, and people got very irritated when they received messages that were of no interest or relevance to them. The system worked fairly well, although there was some cost in terms of my time and lost opportunities for communication.

Other companies have mail areas called "Junk Mail" or "Fourth Class Mail" that employees can use for classified ads, requests for general information, etc. Mail with these designations is usually separated from normal person-to-person mail, so busy people aren't bothered by it. If your company offers this benefit, use it—but follow the organization's rules and check everything twice before you send it out.

Email overload—real

In the *New Yorker* article, Bill Gates is said to spend at least two hours a day reading and responding to his email. I'm surprised it's not more. Many people in business find that they spend half their time or more dealing with email. You can do your part to ease this problem by remembering Rule 4—Respect other people's time—and sending mail only when it needs to be sent.

Don't waste your colleagues' time by copying them on notes that don't affect them. (On the other hand, *do* keep them informed about projects they're working on. Don't assume that they already know what's happening. Remember Felix Unger's injunction: When we assume, we make an ASS out of U and ME.[2])

Don't send email telling people that you put something in their paper in-basket. This is a killer time-waster and rude to boot, since it assumes that the recipient isn't going to read his or her snail mail. If you think the paper you're sending looks so unimportant that no one will read it, attach a paper note explaining why it is important. If it's not important, don't send it.

An exception to this rule might occur when you know that the recipient is a snail-mail ignorer (see below). It's also acceptable to send a short email message alerting someone that you've sent her U.S. mail.

Try not to send a string of related messages in a row because you forgot an important point (e.g., the time or date of a meeting), or resend the same document several times because you corrected an error. Everyone makes mistakes, and one of the great things about electronic communications is that they make correcting errors so simple. But remember that it's easier on your readers (as well as making you look better) if you get it right the first time.

Finally, I believe it was Einstein who said something like "Everything should be made as simple as possible, but no simpler." That goes double for email. Whether you're asking or answering a question, try to

---

2. From the classic TV show "The Odd Couple."

include all the necessary information without wandering or rambling. Actually, the world would be a better place if people followed this advice in all their communications, electronic or not.

Email overload—imagined

A related problem is that of people who don't really receive an outrageous amount of email, but think they do. Some of these people are technophobes who haven't yet figured out that reading their work email is a professional responsibility just like answering their phones. Others just think their own work is so important that they don't have to pay attention to anyone else. I've had the unpleasant experience of sending fairly urgent email to one of these folks, running into the culprit in the hallway later in the day, and being told, "Oh, I had 20 messages in my mailbox this morning so I didn't read any of them."

In case anyone missed the question above "How often should I check my email?" here's the answer again: At least twice a day. The fact that important information comes to you electronically is no excuse for ignoring it—I don't care how busy you are.

If you're stuck working with someone who's not good about reading their email, you have two options:

1. *Don't use email to communicate with them.* Unfortunately, email ignorers are usually equally difficult to reach by traditional methods, so this probably won't work.

2. *CYA.*[3] Use the return receipt feature on your mail system. (Guy Kawasaki hates this feature, but here's one place where it's useful.) If you send important mail and it's not read in a reasonable amount of time, follow up with a phone call. If you still get nowhere, send another email note and copy your own boss (if you just want to keep yourself out of trouble) or the other person's boss (if you want to get the other person in trouble). Warning: Copy a manager only when it's really important that your information get through. It's a technique guaranteed to make you unpopular with the person

3. Cover Your Ass.

you're supposed to be working with, and the boss may see it as evidence that you're not capable of working out your problems on your own. Copying both bosses is almost always overkill.

Snail mail ignorers

Some people get so addicted to their email that they decide they don't need to read their snail mail any more. That's another no-no. The existence of email doesn't excuse you from looking through your paper mailbox regularly—even if 95% of its contents are junk. Check your paper mail at least once a day.

The agony of automatic deletions

Most email isn't stored locally on your workstation; most of it is stored elsewhere in your organization, on a server that's maintained by computer worker bees. This has the advantage to you, the user, of not clogging up your own personal hard disk with mail messages. The server's hard disk gets clogged up instead.

So what's a computer worker bee to do? Simple: Schedule periodic deletions. Where I used to work, all messages over 30 days old were deleted once a month. The computer folks usually gave us plenty of notice, and it was easy enough to save important messages before they were deleted. Easy, that is, if you didn't have hundreds of messages from the last two months to sort through. Or if you didn't forget to deal with them till you were halfway across the country on a trip.

The result of an automatic deletion is that your old email messages—which have supplemented or replaced your paper chron file—disappear. That might be great; there might be messages there that you'd rather have disappear. On the other hand, someday you might want a copy of the note your boss sent you saying "Don't worry about the Furshlugginer project; it's a low priority right now."

What can you do? A number of things:

• Protect yourself: Remember to save copies—on paper, on your own workstation, or both—of your own important email messages.

- Document cases where problems are caused by lost files or deleted email. With a little luck and a lot of caution on your part, these will all happen to other people.

- Lobby within your company for a corporate response to the problem of archiving and backup. Write memos to your boss about the potential dangers of lost files. Get together with like-minded colleagues in an informal working group (not a "committee"; that's a dirty word these days). Produce a report on the potential financial damage to the company from lost records and the cost-effective solutions that could be implemented now, before disaster strikes. Use of your own company's favored jargon will dramatically increase your chances of success.

11. *You, Your Company &*
Cyberspace

Netiquette and company policy

Traditionally, many companies have required their employees to insert a "standard disclaimer" in all email messages they send from their company address. The disclaimer goes something like "these opinions are my own and do not necessarily represent those of XYZCorp." and is often humorously modified to things like "These opinions belong to me, not to my company—they don't want them and they can't have them."[4]

But despite the disclaimer, management at many organizations has the uncomfortable feeling that its employees are representing The Company out there in cyberspace. That is, if management has any awareness at all that cyberspace exists. Interestingly, nobody else in cyberspace believes that. If you work at IBM and you send a note to the USENET newsgroup rec.pets.cats saying "Fleabusters is the best!", no one reading the newsgroup is going to think that Fleabusters has IBM's official

---

4. The disclaimer is often embedded in a "sig file" that automatically appears in every note you send. In fact, the standard disclaimer may have been the reason the sig file was invented.

endorsement, even though the company name appears in your Internet address.

So what are your Netiquette responsibilities as your organization's ambassador to the Net?

That's a tricky question. Many people's only access to the Internet and other network services is through work, and most people use it for something that's not strictly business-related at some point. Historically, most companies have turned a benign blind eye to the situation, as most do to limited personal use of the telephone at work. But as network access becomes more common, more companies will start trying to impose restrictions on how it's used.

Netiquette vs. business etiquette

Many of these questions fall outside the realm of Netiquette. They're really questions of business etiquette and business ethics.

Here's a good example: A large company instituted a drug testing program for new job applicants. One long-time employee disapproved. He called up the director of the program and, over the phone, got a detailed rationale for the program's existence. He then wrote an essay summarizing the rationale and, point by point, demolishing the argument. He posted the essay to a public discussion group. Needless to say, the folks in Public Relations were a little disconcerted when they found out about it.

Did the employee in question break any rules of Netiquette? Assuming that nothing he posted was an outright lie or misrepresentation of the facts, he did not. No one in cyberspace cares whether you follow your company's chain of command.

However, I don't know what repercussions, if any, came back to the fellow from his employer. That Netiquette fails to forbid an activity doesn't make it a good idea.

In summary: Netiquette certainly doesn't forbid the use of work facilities for personal purposes. Nor does it require slavish adherence to company policy. But Netiquette does forbid spreading misinformation, personal or confidential information, or any statement that is needlessly damaging to others—including businesses. What's "needlessly damaging"? That's up to you to decide.

Company privacy policies

An important part of any company's cyberspace policy is its rules on email privacy. See "Email Privacy—a Grand Illusion?" on page 125 for discussion.

Part IV
Social Netiquette

12. *Netiquette at Home*

When you enter cyberspace from home, you probably spend most of your time pursuing activities that are just for fun. As you start getting connected, you may find that you want to spend more and more time in cyberspace. You may find yourself spending less time with your family. If you're a teenager, both you and your family may consider this an advantage. But, in many cases, your family will decide it wants you back.

What to do about this? First of all, never let the computer replace human interaction. Sure, networks are a substitute for face-to-face conversation. We've used substitutes like that for a long time; that's why writing was invented. But even with letters, telephones, videoconferences, and email, we still fly across the country for a meeting occasionally. And you owe your family at least the same courtesy you give your colleagues.

Try to schedule your online time for when others in your family are doing something else. For example, if you live with a sports fan but you can't tell the Bills from the Cowboys, the Superbowl is a great opportunity for some heavy net interaction.

If you're a student, you can always claim to be doing your homework. If you live with your parents, chances are good they'll never figure out what you're up to. Roommates are more likely to catch on, especially if your modem is tying up the phone. If you spend a lot of time logged in, look into getting a second phone line for the modem. A second residential line isn't very expensive and can improve your domestic harmony significantly. It will also prevent those nasty download interruptions that happen when someone else in the house picks up the phone.

Huge phone bills for long-distance modem calls are a major Netiquette no-no unless you pay them yourself. Try to use local access numbers; depending on your type of phone service, these are often a free call.

Finally, if the people you live with are driving you crazy—whether they're your roommates, your parents, your siblings, your spouse, or your significant other—check out the USENET newsgroup alt.flame.roommate. It's guaranteed to bring a nasty smile to the most jaded face.

13. *Netiquette at School*

Cyberspace has the potential to be a tremendous resource for students and teachers at all levels. The Internet was invented as a research tool, and it's been used at universities, especially by graduate students and professors, almost since its inception. Its use is now spreading downward to undergraduates, high school students, and even elementary schools.

And new uses pop up every day. There's a discussion group that functions as a support group for first-year teachers. Other discussion groups allow teachers in the same discipline to exchange ideas and teaching methods. At Monta Vista High School in Cupertino, California, there's a class devoted solely to the Internet. College teachers encourage their students to do their research on the net.

Unfortunately, all this new net traffic can present problems. The Internet was designed for use by adult computer experts, not novices and children. Children, of course, rapidly become computer experts. But the openness of the Internet, which makes it so useful to all users, can also be problematic in several situations. Adults worry that children in the midst of more or less innocent net surfing may stumble across adult material not meant for their eyes. And novices can bombard experts with basic questions (violating Netiquette Rule 4, Respect other people's time).

Fortunately, there's a lot that can be done about these problems.

Kids in cyberspace

Netiquette prescribes no special rules for kids in cyberspace. But following the rules of Netiquette requires a level of maturity that even many adults lack. Additionally, some areas of cyberspace contain material that, in the words of the TV disclaimers, "may be inappropriate for young people." So it's up to adults to introduce kids to cyberspace in a way that is pleasant and productive both for the kids and for the people they meet on the net.

In their article "The Internetworked School: A Policy for the Future," Barry Fishman and Roy Pea address some of these issues.[1] They note that new approaches to teaching often spark community controversy, and that therefore, educators would be well advised to think through possible problems before they put their classrooms online.

Fishman and Pea suggest that any special ground rules for primary and secondary students in cyberspace should be based on existing sets of analogous guidelines. The most important of these is probably the school's existing policy on speech and behavior. They recommend that schools not routinely inspect students' private email or other areas designated as private. However, they do approve of rules against obscene, harassing, or abusive language. Additionally, just as students are expected to behave especially well when they're on "field trips" away from school, they suggest reminding students that they are in effect on a "virtual field trip" when they communicate with others in cyberspace.

I performed a few brief, totally unscientific interviews with some high school Internet users in my neighborhood. These students operate under rules that conform fairly closely to what Fishman and Pea suggest:

- They're forbidden to access any USENET newsgroup or other area of cyberspace that their parents or teachers would disapprove of.

---

1. Printed in *TECHNOS: Quarterly of Education and Technology*, 3(1), pp. 22-26.

They're expected to know what kind of material that includes and to leave the area immediately if they encounter it accidentally.

- They're prohibited from using any form of obscene, harassing, or abusive language online.

- If they break these rules, they lose their school-sponsored Internet accounts.

The students I spoke to didn't mind these restrictions. In fact, when I asked them what net behavior they found most obnoxious, the first thing they mentioned was long, rude, profane, or off-the-topic flaming. Several thought that potentially offensive material should be curtailed to prevent younger children from seeing it. They also felt it was perfectly appropriate for operators of private bulletin boards to remove particularly obnoxious users.

See "Cyberspace Predators" on page page 83 for more on specific dangers to kids in cyberspace.

Knowing whom to ask, or the art of getting help

In *Risks Digest* 15.57, Dan Yurman tells a distressing story about an incident that took place at a major Eastern university.[2] A graduate teaching assistant told a class of undergraduates to use the Internet as a research resource for an assigned paper. The students followed their instructions and fired off a lot of very basic questions (example: "What is hazardous waste?") to a mailing list used mostly by experts to discuss environmental issues.

The rest of the tale is a familiar one of escalating flameage. The experts were annoyed at having their time wasted in this manner. They told the undergraduates to take a walk to the library or look the information up in an almanac. The students and the teaching assistant were surprised, angry, and defensive.

---

2. You can retrieve Yurman's report, entitled "Email Courtesy," from the Red Rock Eater information archive maintained by Phil Agre. Just send email to rre-request@weber.ucsd.edu with the subject line "archive send courtesy".

Yurman interpreted the problem as a failure to follow Netiquette Rule 1, Remember the human. "The root cause appears to be [that] neither the TA nor the students had any idea who was at the other end of the line," he wrote. "All they saw was a computer that should be giving them answers."

Another view is that the teaching assistant and the students were simply reacting to the media hype that has been telling anyone who will listen that cyberspace resources are about to replace books, libraries, librarians, and all other traditional repositories of information. For example, a recent TV commercial for a telecommunications company shows happy and cooperative teenagers in a videoconference learning about the history of jazz from an apparent expert who's connected to them via a voice and video hookup. Of course, the commercial doesn't tell us whether the expert is being paid for his time or who did the work of setting up the cyber-classroom.

A third explanation—along with a solution, thank goodness—has been advanced by Phil Agre. In a tremendously useful article called "The Art of Getting Help," published in his electronic newsletter *The Network Observer*, Agre noted that both the students and the TA displayed a lack of knowledge of where to get help. Agre points out that everyone needs help with research projects, that getting help is a skill, and that this skill is not inborn.[3] I highly recommend retrieving the article (instructions are in the footnote below).

Agre suggests that all students should be taught how to get help before they're turned loose on the Internet. It's the teacher's responsibility to help the student focus a project down to the point where he can start asking for help. The next resources to use are the obvious ones—reference works and research librarians who are in the business of being asked questions.

Agre also points out that we shouldn't "get hung up on the Internet," but should "think of the Internet as simply one part of a larger ecology

---

3. To retrieve Agre's article "The Art of Getting Help," send email to rre-request@weber.ucsd.edu with the subject line "archive send getting-help".

of information sources and communication media." Finally, Agre reminds readers that, since "people aren't obligated to help you," courtesy and care in how you ask your questions will work to your benefit. Wise words for any cyberspace traveler to follow.

14. *Love & Sex in Cyberspace*

Naturally, some people use cyberspace as a venue for romantic encounters. Net romance can take many forms. I know one California woman who, through a series of coincidences, started corresponding electronically with a man in France. Gradually their interest became romantic, and eventually they decided to visit each other's countries and meet in person.

Robin Williams, author of *The Mac Is Not a Typewriter* and other Macintosh books, writes about receiving email from a young man she didn't know. He had searched the profiles in the commercial online service they both used and discovered that they shared an interest in Shakespeare. Despite differences in age, religion, and geographic location, they kept up the correspondence. Eventually they got to know each other better innocently "chatting" in a "private room." "Somehow, over the months," Williams writes, "this unlikely relationship took an unexpected romantic turn."[1]

---

1. In *The Official America Online Membership Kit & Tour Guide*, by Tom Lichty, p. 249.

Cyberspace can also be a great place to carry on an illicit relationship. In Paulina Borsook's short story "Love Over the Wires,"[2] the heroine carries on a torrid epistolary affair with one man while living with another. She can be sitting at her computer writing to her lover, while her official significant other is in the next room.

There are plenty of "adults-only" discussion groups and chat rooms, intended for sex talk rather than romance. And MUDs involve some proportion of sexual activity.

For the most part, romance Netiquette is the same as romance etiquette. Here are a few questions you might ask, however:

Q. Does online cheating count?

Does your nonvirtual significant other know about it and think it's fine? If the answer is yes, you're clear. If the answer is no, it counts.

Q. I've been carrying on a romantic correspondence with someone I've only met online. Recently I've become romantically interested in another electronic friend. Will I be cheating on my original "virtual S. O." if I pursue a romance with another person?

Yes. You owe your online friends the same standards of honor and honesty as your nonvirtual friends.

Q. This person I've only met electronically is pursuing me romantically. I'm not interested. How should I handle it?

Since you don't know the person live, you can't use subtle nonverbal signals to show your lack of interest. But those subtle nonverbal signals don't always work anyway—even in person. You need to move to the next level: directness. Send email saying, "I'm flattered, but I'm just not interested." (*Don't* post the note where others can see it; there's no need to humiliate the unrequited one.) If the person keeps bugging you,

---

2. "Love Over the Wires" by Paulina Borsook, in *Wired* magazine vol. 1.4, September/October 1993.

well, that's what kill files are for. If your system doesn't offer a kill file, lobby with the management to get one.

Things to watch out for

Romance is probably physically safer online than, say, at a downtown bar. It's harder to get beaten up, raped, or infected with an incurable disease when you're communicating via computer.

But cyberspace romance is no safer emotionally than real life. The questions above hint at some of the dangers you might encounter. Here are some stories:

The Net Lothario

In one well-publicized case, a particularly charming fellow was quite successful in romancing women on the WELL. With at least two women, the relationship progressed to the physical level. Through discussion in a women-only area of the WELL, his victims learned they had all been involved with the same guy, and he'd told each one how special and unique she was. Needless to say, they weren't pleased.

Their response: They posted a note to a public forum warning others about the "Cyber-Scam-Artist." They didn't reveal his name in the posting, but offered to give it to anyone who called and asked them.

This response was an example of excellent Netiquette. The women took action to protect other women rather than to get revenge. Their decision not to reveal the cad's name in their posting was especially well-considered. And they seem to have successfully stopped the cad's actions.

However, the cad himself felt his treatment was unfair. Although he admitted he had made mistakes—both by lying and by assuming "that computer relationships were somehow different than physical relationships"—he defended himself by saying that both he and the women had been voluntarily "experimenting in a very new area."[3] That's true, but it's no excuse.

---

3. "He went to the WELL too often," *San Francisco Examiner*, July 13, 1993.

People who misrepresent themselves

The women in the previous story were able to confirm the identity of their Casanova because he'd used his real name with all of them. In fact, while many WELL users have "handles," the WELL doesn't permit users to hide their real names from others. But many other services do. And some people take unfair advantage of that.

As long ago as 1985, *Ms.* magazine reported on the case of "Joan," a mute, crippled, and disfigured neuropsychologist who lived in New York City.[4] "Joan" was a CompuServe user who spent a lot of time in the service's chat area. She developed close friendships with a number of other women on CompuServe. She was known for giving good advice and warm support, especially to other disabled women.

Imagine those women's surprise when they found out that "Joan" was really "Alex," a male psychiatrist who was neither crippled, disfigured nor mute. (However, it's probably safe to assume that he *was* somewhat confused.) It seems that the "Joan" persona began as an experiment for Alex: He wanted to find out what it would be like to be treated as a woman and have female friends. But the experiment became an obsession.

Note the similarity between this story and the previous one: In both cases, the culprits were "experimenting." They believed behavior that would definitely be unacceptable in "real life" might be permissible in cyberspace. Their confusion was understandable. But they were wrong.

Sexual harassment in discussion groups and MUDs

Sexual harassment exists online in many forms. In discussion groups, especially in flame-oriented ones, men often post rude and sexually demeaning messages directed at women. In the unmoderated feminist newsgroups on USENET (alt.feminism and soc.women), it's been estimated that about 80% of the postings are from men, and from my observation, about half of these are anti-feminist.[5] In these groups,

---

4. "The Strange Case of the Electronic Lover" by Lindsy Van Gelder, *Ms.*, October 1985.

unfortunately, the flamers have co-opted the conversation. You pretty much have to go to a moderated discussion group to have an intelligent discussion on feminism.

In some MUDs, a behavior called net.sleazing takes place. Net.sleazing is going around a MUD and soliciting "tinysex," or onscreen sex talk. Extreme sleazes have been known to save these conversations to text files and post them to USENET.

In general, Netiquette frowns on these behaviors. But keep in mind that there are discussion groups, MUDs, and MOOs for every proclivity. Try to be aware of where you are in cyberspace; it may be a place where you don't like the conventions. If that's the case, just leave.

However, harassment is not appropriate in most areas of cyberspace. If you experience it, you have pretty much the same options that you have when you're subjected to a gross-out flame:

- Email the offending party and explain that his/her behavior is not acceptable.

- Email the system operator or system administrator and ask that the offender be censured or disciplined.

- In extreme cases (such as that of the Net Lothario, above), post a complaint or an exposé to the net. Be cautious with this technique, however; you could cause a major flame war.

Pornography in cyberspace

Like the real world, the virtual world contains pornography. And, like real-world etiquette, Netiquette takes no position on pornography's existence.

However, Netiquette recognizes that some people are deeply offended and upset by material that others enjoy. Therefore, those who enjoy

---

5. Statistic from "Gender Issues in Computer Networking" by Leslie Regan Shade, McGill University.

pornography have the responsibility to be considerate of those who don't.

If you are posting pornographic or erotic material, it's your responsibility to make sure no one stumbles on it by accident. First of all, post it in the right place—that is, in an area that is clearly marked as containing material of a sexual nature. Never post pornography or erotica to an area of cyberspace that is frequented by children. And never post material just for the purpose of being offensive, unless you're posting it to an area that exists for the purpose of being offensive (alt.tasteless, for example).

If you're using a UNIX newsreading system, you can probably "rotate" your messages. "Rotation" is an easy way to encrypt messages so that they're easy to decrypt, but can't be read by accident. The standard method, called "rot13," rotates each letter by thirteen characters so that an "a" becomes an "n." For example, the word "sex" would appear as "frk."

You might use rot13 encryption if, for example, you wanted to post a dirty joke to a humor discussion group that also contains innocent knock-knock jokes.[6] (Although there should probably be two separate groups for the two different kinds of humor.) When you use rot13 encryption, be sure to put the word "rot13" in the subject line of the message. Your system administrator should be able to help you if you want more information.

Pornography and copyright

Various areas of cyberspace contain erotic pictures that anyone can download. Many of these pictures are scanned from copyrighted magazines like *Playboy* and *Penthouse.* That's a copyright violation. And copyright violations are very bad Netiquette, regardless of the subject matter. So please don't upload or download graphics created by artists

---

6. Rot13 encryption can also be used when posting a "spoiler"—a note that reveals the ending of, for example, a movie or novel.

who haven't given permission for electronic distribution of their work. See "Copyright in Cyberspace" on page 133 for more.

Part V

Legal & Philosophical Issues in Netiquette

15. *Email Privacy—a Grand Illusion?*

When you send an email message to a friend, you probably assume that random people won't be reading it. You could be right. But don't count on it.

Why not? First of all, most email is sent in the form of plain ASCII text, which means humans can read it. Encrypted text, on the other hand, requires a key or a supercomputer to decode into human-readable form.

Second, every email system has administrators who have unlimited access to all mail messages sent from, to, and through that system. It's possible to design a system that doesn't have this feature, but there aren't many. In fact, when you send an email message across the Internet, it often hops from server to server several times before it reaches its destination. As a result, it can be read by system administrators all across the country—possibly the world.

This isn't necessarily a bad thing. To make a system work, the sysadmin needs this kind of power. If a message is incorrectly addressed, the sysadmin can open it up and figure out who should get it. If messages get garbled, the sysadmin may be able to restore them. If you forget your password, the sysadmin can do a "reset" and give you a new one.

A system administrator with any sense of ethics—or even one who's reasonably busy—won't routinely read other people's mail. But it's not a safe assumption that all sysadmins are too honest or too overworked to snoop.[1]

The privacy problem extends beyond nosy sysadmins. The technology needed to automatically screen large volumes of email is widely available.[2] Sometimes, as a matter of company policy, businesses routinely screen employees' email. To make matters worse, agencies of the federal government can readily monitor vast quantities of email, automatically searching for key words.

Perhaps even more common than active snooping is human error. Here are some of the things that can happen:

- You accidentally send your note to the person about whom you wrote unflattering things in the message. (Don't laugh, I've seen it happen.)

- The person who received your note forwards it to the person about whom you wrote unflattering things. (I've seen this one too.)

- You accidentally send your message to an international mailing list, rather than a private recipient. (Be careful when using the "reply" feature in response to mailing list messages.)

- You save your racy email messages in a text file on your Mac. Then, unthinking, you publish your Mac to the network as a server. Any network cruiser who cares can now find out exactly what kind of underwear you think is sexy. (Again, I am not making this up.)

---

1. However, the last thing I want to do is cast aspersions on system administrators as a group. In general, sysadmins are overworked and underrecognized. Be nice to your system adminstrator and she'll be nice to you.
2. Any UNIX sysadmin worth his salt can use the *grep* command to concoct a simple script to search all incoming and outgoing mail.

The prescription for these ills is twofold:

1. Understand how your email system and network are set up, and just who can see what.

2. Don't do stupid things.

Unfortunately, etiquette books can't eliminate human carelessness. So, just as the only 100% effective form of birth control is abstinence, you could prevent breaches of privacy by refusing to use email. For most of us, however, neither remedy holds much attraction. A fallback remedy is to follow your grandmother's advice: Never put anything in writing that you wouldn't mind seeing on the front page of the *New York Times*.

Of course, the rule of etiquette is the same for email as for old-fashioned letters: Never, ever snoop in another person's papers.

Company policies on email content and privacy

The Electronic Communications Privacy Act (ECPA) of 1986 makes it illegal to intercept electronic messages sent over public systems (for example, America Online or MCI Mail) without a search warrant. But the law doesn't address the privacy rights of employees whose email accounts are provided by their employers. Even in states like California, where citizens have a constitutional right to privacy, the rules aren't clear. That leaves the legal ball in the court of the company policy.

But few companies have policies on corporate email. The email policies that exist address the content, distribution, and privacy of email. Privacy policies range from "Management can read any message any time for any reason" to "No one looks at anyone else's mail. Period." Rules on the contents can be as restrictive as "Email is to be used for business-related communication only" or as open as "Email may be used for personal purposes at will."

The best of these policies reserve the company's right to examine email for legitimate business purposes, but forbid any unauthorized person to read or intercept another person's mail. They usually allow personal use within reason, operating on the assumption that if an employee spends all his time writing long personal email messages, his manager will probably notice that he isn't getting his job done and do something about it.

A case study: Borland vs. Symantec

For those who are interested, here's a story about an employer-employee privacy conflict that made it into the papers:

About two years ago, Eugene Wang, a vice president at the software company Borland International, left for rival firm Symantec. After Wang left, former colleagues at Borland checked his MCI Mail account—which Borland had paid for—and discovered messages sent to Symantec while Wang was a Borland employee, containing what Borland said were trade secrets. Wang's response was that (1) Borland had no right to check his MCI Mail account and (2) they weren't trade secrets anyway. Borland claims a written policy that gave the organization the right to search company property for company information gave them the right to read the messages. Both Wang and Symantec president Gordon Eubanks were named in a lawsuit by Borland, still unresolved when *Netiquette* went to press.

When last heard from, Symantec had instituted an email policy forbidding employees to use company email for personal purposes. Borland still didn't have a specific email policy.

What to do about it

In general, Netiquette supports the existence of company email policies. A written policy can protect you from, for example, being fired because your boss was snooping on your email and read the derogatory note you wrote about him to your friend across the hall. (Yes, this has really happened.) And it lets everyone know the organization's expectations for how email should be used. However, company policies can also be unnecessarily restrictive.

If you're interested in helping your organization set up an email policy, you could contact the Electronic Messaging Association (EMA), which represents email suppliers and corporate users. The EMA sells "Access to and Use and Disclosure of Electronic Mail on Company Computer

Systems: A Tool Kit for Formulating Your Company's Policy." It's $45 and is available from EMA at (703) 524-5550.

But be warned: The EMA's position on privacy is that "employers need the right to control, evaluate, and monitor all forms of employee communication." EMA director William Moroney has stated that corporate email users shouldn't expect "any more right of privacy than they get from tossing a memo in their out-basket."[3]

Encryption: privacy protection or national security threat?

There is a way to protect your private email from snoopers. It's called encryption. Just as army dispatches during wartime are coded in case they fall into the wrong hands, it's technically possible to code, or encrypt, email messages. The technologies and techniques vary. But, for a variety of political reasons, built-in encryption has not been widely deployed in email systems.

The lack of a widely deployed encryption system has held back the commercial growth of the Internet. This is ironic given that several practically unbreakable systems are available. One very promising concept is called "public-key encryption." To grossly oversimplify, with this encryption system, everyone has two encryption keys: One is public, the other is private. I send my public key to anyone who wants it, but I alone keep my private key.

Here's where it gets really cool. If you wanted to send me a secure message, you would encrypt it with my public key. The message sent over the wires would be indecipherable jargon. When I received it, I'd decrypt it with my private key. For arcane reasons beyond my understanding, this actually works, even though the two keys are different. Only I could decrypt a message that was encrypted with my public key.

Similarly, a message I encrypted with my private key could be decrypted only with my public key. That doesn't make the message

---

3. "Privacy Act would force firms to inform their employees about E-mail monitoring," in *PC Week—Special Report on Workplace Privacy,* June 28, 1993.

secure, since my public key would be available to anyone who wanted it. But it would give my email an unforgeable "digital signature."[4]

This system works because my private key never leaves my grasp. No more nightmares about the code book falling into the hands of the enemy.

But here, the government gets into the act. The intelligence and law enforcement branches of the United States government—the National Security Agency (NSA), the Central Intelligence Agency (CIA), the Federal Bureau of Investigation (FBI), and the Justice and Treasury departments—don't want U.S. citizens using encryption systems they can't break. They claim it's a national security risk and that unbreakable encryption would be a boon to child pornographers. The government has proposed its own encryption scheme—called Clipper—which is being developed specifically so that government agencies will keep copies of everyone's keys.

You could legitimately ask why anyone cares that much about the security of their private communications. After all, what email do you send that it would be *that* big a deal for someone else to see? And anyway, why would anyone *want* to read your mail? But privacy-advocacy groups point out that the government doesn't have a great record of using its surveillance powers wisely. Think back to the McCarthy communist-hunts of the 1950s and the disruption of political groups in the 1960s. More recently, we had the "war on drugs" of the 1980s, which gave state and federal governments extremely broad rights of property seizure.

Historically, these weapons have been used against poor people, minorities, and social and political activists. Perhaps you're sure you'll never fall into any of these groups. For myself—although I'm generally in favor of having a government—I'm not sure I want all of my communications to be an open book to the FBI. In addition, the existence of a

---

4. For an explanation of how all this works, see Bruce Schneier's *Applied Cryptography* (NY: John Wiley & Sons, 1994).

well-publicized "back door" increases the probability that criminals or other unauthorized users will find a way to break in.

Furthermore, as Phil Zimmerman[5] has pointed out, if most people sent all their letters on postcards, anyone who used an envelope would look suspicious. The fact that most of us use envelopes most of the time increases our reasonable expectation of privacy in our written communications.

Finally, keep in mind that in the near future all kinds of personal information will be transmitted over the net, or the National Information Infrastructure (NII). While you may not care now whether your casual email is read, you may care when your credit card records, medical records, and tax returns are transmitted electronically.

On the other hand, I don't want to minimize the dangers of unbreakable encryption. There are people in the world who will use any tool at their disposal to get away with doing bad things. If you're concerned about these issues, consider joining the Electronic Frontier Foundation, a privacy advocacy group started by Mitch Kapor and John Perry Barlow.[6]

Netiquette isn't ready yet to make a call on proper encryption behavior. But one thing is beyond question: Government intrusion into private email is *very bad Netiquette.*

---

5. Phil Zimmerman created PGP, or "Pretty Good Privacy," an implementation of the public-key encryption concept for personal computers. PGP is currently embroiled in a patent dispute and availability of its freeware version is limited.
6. You can contact the EFF at info@eff.org or 202-347-5400.

16. *Copyright in Cyberspace*

Warning and disclaimer

Netiquette rules listed here are suggestions for helping people get along better; they carry no force of law. Explanations of U.S. copyright law in this chapter are a layperson's interpretation and are here for educational purposes only. I am not a lawyer, and nothing in this chapter should be construed as legal advice. Additionally, the interpretation of copyright law changes all the time, so anything in print here may have changed by the time you read it. If you need legal advice, talk to a lawyer!

Some basic information on copyright

This is an extremely basic introduction to the complex subject of copyright. For more detailed information, let me recommend the excellent copyright FAQ by Terry Carroll, available by anonymous FTP from rtfm.mit.edu.[1]

---

1. Connect with server rtfm.mit.edu and look for the directory called /pub/usenet/ news.answers/law/Copyright-FAQ, files part1–part6. Or try ftp.cni.org, in directory /CNI/forums/cni-copyright/other/FAQ. You can also obtain a copy via email. Start by sending a message to mail-server@rtfm.mit.edu with the command "help" in the body.

Q. What is copyright?

What we call "copyright" is really a collection of rights that belong to the creator of an original work—for example, a book, an article, a painting, or a recording. U.S. copyright law recognizes seven of these rights, among them

- the right to reproduce the work
- the right to produce derivative works
- the right to perform the work in public

The purpose of copyright law is to promote the "useful arts" by ensuring that the person who creates an "original work" can benefit from it. The law requires a copyrighted work to be expressed in a "fixed and tangible" form—in other words, you can't copyright a song you've sung or a story you've told but never written down. Material that you've saved to a disk or posted to a discussion group would probably be considered "fixed and tangible," although, to be on the safe side, it couldn't hurt to print a copy to paper.

Copyright is only available for "original works"—that is, things you've created yourself. You can't reprint a Shakespeare sonnet, which is in the public domain (see page 136), and copyright it in your own name.

Q. Why should I care about copyright?

You're likely to care about copyright in two situations:

1. You're producing an original work and want to know what information you can legitimately take from other sources.

2. You've completed the work and want to keep others from infringing your rights to it.

Q. How do I get a copyright on something I've written?

Congratulations! You probably already have it. Thanks to the Berne Convention of 1988, writers and artists in the United States automatically own the copyright to any work they create the moment it is created (with certain exceptions, of course—you didn't expect this to be simple!). By current law, copyright begins when the work is created and is in effect for the duration of the author's life plus 50 years.

You aren't required to put a copyright notice on the work or register it with the U.S. Copyright Office, although there may be good reasons to do so.

Q. OK, I'll bite. Why would I want to?

You might want to register a work with the U. S. Copyright Office because you can only bring a lawsuit for infringement on a work that's registered. And since registering a work only costs $20, the rule of thumb is that you should register any work that's potentially worth more than $20 to you.

You probably wouldn't want to go to the expense and trouble of registering every article or letter you write, however. But just putting a copyright notice on a work may protect some of your rights. More important, it serves as notice to readers that you do care about your copyright and you don't want your work copied, stolen, borrowed, or otherwise abused.

Q. Wait—does that mean I can't write a research paper without violating someone's copyright?

No, don't worry. Copyright only applies to the *expression* of an idea or fact; you can't copyright the idea or fact itself. So you can safely use the fact that cats have three eyelids in your research, even though you read it in a copyrighted newspaper article or looked it up in a copyrighted encyclopedia.

You can also quote directly as long as you follow the rather murky rules of "fair use." The doctrine of "fair use" allows people who don't hold the copyright to a work to use portions of that work anyway. The doctrine's purpose is to keep copyright laws from stifling the very creativity they were designed to protect. For writers, the doctrine of fair use generally permits quotation of short excerpts of a work in a review or criticism, in a scholarly or technical work, or in a parody. A use is more likely to be considered "fair" if it's for educational or nonprofit purposes and if the resulting product doesn't compete with the original work.

Please note that this is a *very* cursory discussion of the concept of fair use. Check out the Copyright FAQ for more information.

Copyright and posted material

The free exchange of information through cyberspace has raised all sorts of questions about who owns that material. Is material that's posted to a discussion group still owned by the original author? What if it's repeatedly quoted in further discussion? What if you write a FAQ and make it publicly available—do you still own the copyright?

The answer to these questions is yes, yes, and yes. If it's your original work and you wrote it down, the copyright is yours.

There's a common—and mistaken—belief that posting information to USENET, or anywhere else in cyberspace, puts it in the public domain. That's not true. Think about it—if you paint a picture and display it for all to see, you're not giving up the copyright to it.

Q. What's the public domain?

Anything that's not under copyright is in the public domain. That means anyone can freely copy and distribute it. You can give copies away for free, or, if anyone's willing to pay, you can charge them.

As of 1994, most works created before 1922 are out of copyright and in the public domain. An author can also choose to put a work into the public domain by declaring, in writing, that he is doing so. That doesn't apply to most of the material that's posted in cyberspace. So most of the posted material you see—whether it's a note in a discussion group or an article whose author is seeking comments—is under copyright and belongs to the author.

Q. Does that mean I have to stop quoting other people's messages in my discussion group postings?

No. When you post to USENET—or anywhere where quoting and forwarding of messages is common—you are probably giving an "implied license" to quote and forward. In any case, because quoting and forwarding are customary on public discussion groups, you should expect anything you post there to be quoted and/or forwarded within the discussion group.

Q. I'm writing an article for publication. Can I use quotations from individuals' discussion group postings in it?

Probably nothing bad would happen to you if you did. But it's better Netiquette to ask for permission. Postings from individuals aren't usually carefully thought out; they represent the individual's feelings and opinions at a given moment. Think how you'd feel if a comment you made in a bar after a few beers turned up in the paper the next day.

Q. What if an email note of mine gets written up in the Washington Post*?*

This would be extremely bad Netiquette. Unfortunately, it's completely possible. In fact, in one unfortunate case, it's happened. Newspapers around the country are plugging into the net. Their reporters go "net trawling" for stories. The reporters hang out in smoky dens, mailing lists that only accept professional journalists, and exchange leads. While conscientious reporters try to contact their sources before running a story, they don't have to, and sometimes they don't. If they use your message as material, they're protected by the First Amendment.

Q. Can I use email a friend sent me to bolster my position in an argument I'm pursuing in a discussion group?

Don't do it without permission. Posting private email to the net without the author's OK is considered very poor Netiquette.

Q. I've found a FAQ that covers a lot of the territory I'm writing about in this article. Can I use it?

You can certainly refer to the FAQ, cite facts from it, and quote it within reason. But you can't legally reproduce large parts of it without the author's permission. After all, the author may want to publish it himself or herself one day. Unfortunately, the legal limit on how large a part you can use is set only by the ill-defined doctrine of fair use. So you just have to use your best judgment.

Q. This FAQ is so great, I want to pass it on to my mom. Is that OK?

Yes, that's fine. FAQs are posted for everyone to use. But be sure to include the copyright notice in any copies you spread around, either on paper or electronically.[2]

Q. In my research, I discovered that the FAQ contains some errors. Can I correct them in the copy I'm sending my mom?

No. It's very bad Netiquette to modify another person's work. Email a polite note to the author of the FAQ explaining the error you found. Chances are that if you're correct, the author will want to use your information. You can send a separate note to your mom, as well.

Q. I just got a scanner, and I want to give something back to the cyberspace community. Is it OK if I scan cartoons out of the New Yorker *and upload them for others to enjoy?*

No, no, no! Your desire to share is commendable. But either the *New Yorker* or the original artist owns the copyright to those cartoons, and whichever one of them owns it probably plans to keep it.

---

2. Some FAQs and related documents can be copied electronically but not printed without paying a license fee. Erik J. Heels' wonderful "Legal List" works this way. (It's available via FTP at ftp.cni.org, directory /CNI/forums/cni-copyright/other/ FAQ/legallist.txt).

Q. But why shouldn't I? Who would it hurt?

Good question. In the short run, maybe it wouldn't hurt anyone. But remember that copyright law exists to encourage the "useful arts" by ensuring that artists profit from their creations. If you upload those cartoons and give them away for free, and later the *New Yorker* decides to create its own for-profit online service that offers cartoon downloading, your action would have affected their potential market. And, at least in theory, that could ultimately discourage the *New Yorker* from printing cartoons at all, which would be a sad day for everyone.

In addition, if the folks at the *New Yorker* get wind of your activity, they might not take it kindly. And they might have the resources to sue you and make your life very unpleasant.

In summary, remember: Copyright isn't just good Netiquette—it's the law.

The promise of Xanadu (it'll be ready in 6 months)

You may have heard of Xanadu or of Ted Nelson. Nelson, a certified Brilliant Guy, came up with the idea for Xanadu in the early 1960s. Ever since then, he's been swearing it's going to be available in six months.

But whether or not Xanadu ever comes to fruition, it's a really interesting idea. Among other things, it's a technical solution to the legal and ethical problem of maintaining copyright in cyberspace.

Xanadu would be—or will be—a huge repository of published information. It could contain anything—music, reference material, stories, movies, you name it. Users would connect to it from outside and read or download as much or as little information as they liked. And—here's the really clever part—users would *automatically* be charged for their usage, and a royalty would *automatically* go to the author.

There's a lot more to Xanadu than that. If you're interested, I recommend Nelson's 1974 book *Computer Lib/Dream Machines,* which was reissued by Microsoft Press in 1987.

Conclusion: Whither Netiquette?

There's a famous paper called "The Tragedy of the Commons"—so famous that referencing it is almost a cliché all by itself. In this paper, economist Garrett Hardin talks about the village commons, a grassy area where sheep graze. The sheep are owned by individuals, but the commons belongs to everyone in the village.

According to Hardin, it's inevitable that one person, motivated by the completely reasonable desire for profit, will put too many sheep on the commons, resulting in overgrazing. This person starts underselling his neighbors, who have the choice of joining him in the abuse of a common resource or going out of business. In the short run a few people maximize their profit, but in the long run the commons is ruined for everyone.

Today, cyberspace is a commons. Many, many people have access to it at little or no direct cost; it's supported by private enterprise and tax dollars. And the many people who pay no per-message charges for email could easily start "overgrazing" the Internet by, for example, sending out huge numbers of messages to huge numbers of users.

This book is one attempt to hedge against the tragedy of the commons. But, by itself, it's powerless. The rules of Netiquette can only work if they're adopted by a majority of the people in cyberspace—if they become a community standard.

In *The Network Observer* of March 1994, Phil Agre discusses the need for community standards, as well as the need to promulgate them by telling stories. When someone does something really obnoxious on the net, tell your cyberspace friends about it. When someone does something really great, tell a story about that too. As the stories spread, so will the principles they embody. And as people come to understand and accept the principles, Netiquette will become second nature to them.

Bibliography

Most of these works are listed here because I actually refer to them in *Netiquette*, or because they provided important background material. Others are listed because I think they'd be useful references for someone getting started in cyberspace, or just because they're fun to read. The bibliography is divided into printed works and works available online. All the online materials listed are available on the Internet via email or anonymous FTP, and the information necessary to retrieve them is provided.

Have fun!

Printed Works

Barlow, John Perry. "The Economy of Ideas: A framework for rethinking patents and copyrights in the digital age." *Wired* 2.03, March 1994.

Borsook, Paulina. "Love Over the Wires." *Wired* 1.4, September/October 1993.

Gibson, William. *Neuromancer.* New York: Ace Science Fiction Books, 1984.

Godin, Seth. *The Smiley Dictionary.* Berkeley: Peachpit Press, 1993.

Hafner, Katie, and John Markoff. *Cyberpunk: Outlaws and Hackers on the Computer Frontier.* New York: Touchstone (Simon & Schuster), 1991.

Kawasaki, Guy. *The Macintosh Way.* Glenview, IL: Scott, Foresman, and Company, 1990.

---. *The Computer Curmudgeon.* Hayden, 1992.

Krol, Ed. *The Whole Internet User's Guide and Catalog.* Sebastopol, CA: O'Reilly & Associates, Inc., 1992.

LaQuey, Tracey, with Jeanne C. Ryer. *The Internet Companion: A Beginner's Guide to Global Networking.* Reading, MA: Addison-Wesley Publishing Company, 1993.

Levy, Steven. "Crypto-Rebels." *Wired* 1.2, July 1993.

Lichty, Tom. *The Official America Online Membership Kit and Tour Guide.* Chapel Hill, NC: Ventana Press, 1992.

Marine, Craig. "He went to the WELL too often: Cyber-Casanova's women cry wolf on 'Lectronic Link." *San Francisco Examiner*, July 13, 1993.

Martin, Judith. *Miss Manners' Guide to Excruciatingly Correct Behavior.* New York: Warner Books, 1979.

---. *Miss Manners' Guide to Rearing Perfect Children.* New York: Atheneum, 1984.

---. *Miss Manners' Guide for the Turn-of-the-Millennium.* New York: Pharos Books, 1989.

Michael Wolff & Company, Inc. *NetGuide.* New York: Random House Electronic Publishing, 1994.

Nelson, Ted. *Computer Lib/Dream Machines.* Redmond, WA: Tempus Books of Microsoft Press, 1987.

PC Week—Special Report on Workplace Privacy, June 28, 1993. "Electronic monitoring raises legal and societal questions" by Laura B. Smith, and "Privacy Act would force firms to inform their employees about E-mail monitoring" by Richard A. Danca.

Quarterman, John S. *The Matrix: Computer Networks and Conferencing Systems Worldwide.* Bedford, MA: Digital Press, 1990.

Raymond, Eric, ed. *The New Hacker's Dictionary.* Cambridge, MA: The MIT Press, 1991.

Rheingold, Howard. *The Virtual Community: Homesteading on the Electronic Frontier.* Reading, MA: Addison-Wesley Publishing Company, 1993.

Sanderson, David, compiler. *Smileys.* Sebastopol, CA: O'Reilly & Associates, Inc., 1993.

Schneier, Bruce. *Applied Cryptography.* New York: John Wiley & Sons, 1994.

Schrage, Michael. "Manager's Journal: Robert's Rules of Electronic Order." *Wall Street Journal,* November 29, 1993.

Seabrook, John. "A Reporter at Large: E-Mail from Bill." The *New Yorker,* January 10, 1994.

Van Gelder, Lindsy. "The Strange Case of the Electronic Lover." *Ms.,* October 1985.

Works Available Online

Agre, Phil. "The Art of Getting Help." *The Network Observer*, Vol. 1, No. 2, February 1994. Send email to rre-request@weber.ucsd.edu with the subject line "archive send getting-help".

---. "The Internet as a Commons." *The Network Observer*, Vol. 1, No. 3, March 1994. Send email to rre-request@weber.ucsd.edu with the subject line "archive send tno-march-1994".

---. "Networking On the Network." Send email to rre-request@weber.ucsd.edu with the subject line "archive send network".

Note: You can also subscribe to Agre's incredibly useful Red Rock Eater News Service. For information about the email service and how to subscribe, send a message to the server at rre-request@weber.ucsd.edu with the subject line "help".

Carroll, Terry. Copyright FAQ. Available via FTP from rtfm.mit.edu: pub/usenet/news.answers/Copyright-FAQ, files part1-part6. Or from ftp.cni.org, in directory /CNI/forums/cni-copyright/other/FAQ. You can also obtain a copy via email. Start by sending a message to mail-server@rtfm.mit.edu with the command "help" in the body.

Shade, Leslie Regan. "Gender Issues in Computer Networking." Talk given at Community Networking: The International Free-Net Conference, Carleton University, Ottawa, Canada, August 17-19, 1993. Available via FTP from alfred.carleton.ca: pub/freenet/93conference, file leslie_regan_shade.txt.

USENET articles maintained by Gene Spafford:

"What is Usenet?" (original author Chip Salzenberg, edited by Gene Spafford)

"Rules for posting to Usenet" (original author Mark Horton, enhanced & edited by Gene Spafford and Mark Brader)

"A Primer on How to Work With the Usenet Community" (by Chuq Von Rospach, enhanced & edited by Gene Spafford)

"A Brief Guide to Social Newsgroups and Mailing Lists (by Dave Taylor)

"Emily Postnews Answers Your Questions on Netiquette" (by Brad Templeton)

All these incredibly useful articles are regularly posted to the USENET newsgroup news.announce.newusers.

Index

Colophon

Cover design by Jennie Birch
Layout by Seth Ross
Composed on a NeXT Computer running FrameMaker
Printed & bound at Olympian Graphics

Registration Form
Albion Reader Program

❑   Yes, I enjoyed *Netiquette*. Please send me a free catalog of your forthcoming titles and information about discounts on other Albion books.

❑   Yes, I'm interested in receiving current information about the topic of Netiquette via email. Please send me information about subscribing to Albion's Netiquette mailing list. My email address is below.

Return this form via:

❑   fax   +1 415-752-5417

❑   mail   Albion Reader Program
            PO Box 590594
            San Francisco, CA 94159-0594

❑   email readers@albion.com

Name _____

Title _____

Organization _____

Address _____

City_____State_____Zip_____

Country _____

Email address _____

Albion Books   info@albion.com

"Computer books for a converging world"

—